Math Reference for Middle Grades

BY
KARISE MACE AND BARBIE PILLA

COPYRIGHT © 2008 Mark Twain Media, Inc.

ISBN 978-1-58037-448-4

Printing No. CD-404089

Mark Twain Media, Inc., Publishers
Distributed by Carson-Dellosa Publishing LLC

Visit us at www.carsondellosa.com

The purchase of this book entitles the buyer to reproduce the student pages for classroom use only. Other permissions may be obtained by writing Mark Twain Media, Inc., Publishers.

All rights reserved. Printed in the United States of America.

Table of Contents

Table of Contents (cont.)

Letter From the Authors

We are delighted that you have purchased the *Math Reference for Middle School* book. We have written this book so that it is easily accessible to students, teachers, and parents. The book is divided into nine different units covering the topics that are taught as a part of most middle school math curriculums. A unit is divided into several lessons, each of which covers one or two concepts.

You will notice that each lesson is made up of two or three parts. The first part, called "Here's the Info...", provides a step-by-step guide of how to solve problems in that particular content area. Here you will find examples and thorough explanations. The last part, called "Show what you know!", provides practice problems so that you can apply what you have learned. Some lessons contain an intermediate part called "Possible Pitfalls." In this part of the lesson, we have highlighted common mistakes students make.

Throughout the book, you will notice that some of the words are underlined, bolded, and italicized. These words can be found in the glossary. These terms are most often defined in the lesson where they are introduced. However, we have also highlighted them in other lessons to remind you that their definitions can be found in the glossary if you need them.

Units 6 and 7 contain reference pages with important information that is not addressed in an individual lesson.

We have also provided an alignment to show you how this book addresses the NCTM standards.

An accompanying CD-ROM features two printable activities for each lesson that can be used for enrichment or extra practice. A quick-reference sheet for math symbols and geometric figures is also included on the CD-ROM

We certainly hope you will find this book to be helpful in your study of mathematics!

Mathematically yours,

Karise Mace and Barbie Pilla

Alignment to NCTM Standards

Expectations	Lessons
Number and Operations Standard	
Students should understand numbers, ways of representing numbers, relationships among numbers, and number systems.	
• Students should work flexibly with fractions, decimals, and percents to solve problems.	1–4, 14–26, 30–33
• Students should understand and use ratios and proportions to represent quantitative relationships.	27–29
• Students should develop an understanding of large numbers and recognize and appropriately use exponential, scientific, and calculator notation.	8, 11
• Students should use factors, multiples, prime factorization, and relatively prime numbers to solve problems.	5–7
Students should understand meanings of operations and how they relate to one another.	
• Students should understand the meaning and effects of arithmetic operations with fractions, decimals, and integers.	1–4, 16–26, 34–37
• Students should understand and use the inverse relationships of addition and subtraction, multiplication and division, and squaring and finding square roots to simplify computations and solve problems.	47, 54–56, 60–61
Students should compute fluently and make reasonable estimates.	
• Students should develop and analyze algorithms for computing with fractions, decimals, and integers and develop fluency in their use.	1–4, 16–26, 34–37
• Students should develop, analyze, and explain methods for solving problems involving proportions, such as scaling and finding equivalent ratios.	14, 27–29
Algebra Standard	
Students should understand patterns, relations, and functions	
• Students should relate and compare different forms of representation for a relationship.	57, 59
• Students should identify functions as linear or nonlinear and contrast their properties from tables, graphs, or equations.	57, 59

Reprinted with permission from *Principles and Standards for School Mathematics,* copyright 2006 by the National Council of Teachers of Mathematics. All rights reserved.

Standards are listed with the permission of the National Council of Teachers of Mathematics (NCTM). NCTM does not endorse the content or validity of these alignments.

Alignment to NCTM Standards (cont.)

Expectations	Lessons
Algebra Standard (cont.)	
Students should represent and analyze mathematical situations and structures using algebraic symbols.	
• Students should develop an initial conceptual understanding of different uses of variables.	12–13
• Students should explore relationships between symbolic expressions and graphs of lines, paying particular attention to the meaning of intercept and slope.	57–58
• Students should recognize and generate equivalent forms for simple algebraic expressions and solve linear equations.	12–13, 54–56, 60–61
Geometry Standard	
Students should analyze characteristics and properties of two- and three-dimensional geometric shapes and develop mathematical arguments about them.	
• Students should precisely describe, classify, and understand relationships among types of two- and three-dimensional objects using their defined properties.	U6 Ref. Pgs.
• Students should understand relationships among the angles, side lengths, perimeters, areas, and volumes of similar objects.	29, 47–49
• Students should create and critique inductive and deductive arguments concerning geometric ideas and relationships, such as congruence, similarity, and the Pythagorean theorem.	U6 Ref. Pgs., 47
Students should specify locations and describe spatial relationships using coordinate geometry and other representational systems.	
• Students should use coordinate geometry to represent and examine the properties of geometric shapes.	U6 Ref. Pgs.
Students should apply transformations and use symmetry to analyze mathematical situations.	
• Students should describe sizes, positions, and orientations of shapes under informal transformations such as flips, turns, slides, and scaling.	U6 Ref. Pgs.
• Students should examine the congruence, similarity, and line or rotational symmetry of objects using transformations.	U6 Ref. Pgs.
Students should visualize, use spatial reasoning, and geometric modeling to solve problems.	
• Students should use two-dimensional representations of three-dimensional objects to visualize and solve problems such as those involving surface area and volume.	38–49

Reprinted with permission from *Principles and Standards for School Mathematics,* copyright 2006 by the National Council of Teachers of Mathematics. All rights reserved.

Standards are listed with the permission of the National Council of Teachers of Mathematics (NCTM). NCTM does not endorse the content or validity of these alignments.

Alignment to NCTM Standards (cont.)

Expectations	Lessons
Measurement Standard	
Students should understand measurable attributes of objects and the units, systems, and processes of measurement.	
• Students should understand both metric and customary systems of measurement.	U6 Ref. Pgs.
• Students should understand relationships among units and convert from one unit to another within the same system.	U6 Ref. Pgs.
• Students should understand, select, and use units of appropriate size and type to measure angles, perimeter, surface area, and volume.	U6 Ref. Pgs., 38–46
Students should apply appropriate techniques, tools, and formulas to determine measurements.	
• Students should select and apply techniques and tools to accurately find length, area, volume, and angle measures to appropriate levels of precision.	38–46, 48–49
• Students should develop and use formulas to determine the circumference of circles and the area of triangles, parallelograms, trapezoids, and circles and develop strategies to find the area of more-complex shapes.	38–45
• Students should develop strategies to determine the surface area and volume of selected prisms, pyramids, and cylinders.	44–46
• Students should solve problems involving scale factors, using ratio and proportion.	29
Data Analysis and Probability Standard	
Students should formulate questions that can be addressed with data and collect, organize, and display relevant data to answer them.	
• Students should select, create, and use appropriate graphical representations of data, including histograms, box plots, and scatterplots.	U7 Ref. Pgs., 51
Students should select and use appropriate statistical methods to analyze data.	
• Students should find, use, and interpret measures of center and spread, including mean and interquartile range.	50
• Students should discuss and understand the correspondence between data sets and their graphical representations, especially histograms, stem-and-leaf plots, box plots, and scatterplots.	U7 Ref. Pgs.
Students should understand and apply basic concepts of probability.	
• Students should understand and use appropriate terminology to describe complementary and mutually exclusive events.	53
• Students should compute probabilities for simple compound events, using such methods as organized lists, tree diagrams, and area models.	51–53

Reprinted with permission from *Principles and Standards for School Mathematics,* copyright 2006 by the National Council of Teachers of Mathematics. All rights reserved.

Standards are listed with the permission of the National Council of Teachers of Mathematics (NCTM). NCTM does not endorse the content or validity of these alignments.

Name: _____ Date: _____

Unit 1: Decimals

Lesson 1: Adding Decimals

Here's the Info...

Adding decimals can be easy! Find the **_sum_** of 12.36 and 4.12.

Step 1:   Line up the decimal points.

$$\begin{array}{r} 12.36 \\ +\ 4.12 \\ \hline \end{array}$$

Step 2:   Bring down the decimal point.

Step 3:   Add.

$$\begin{array}{r} 12.36 \\ +\ 4.12 \\ \hline 16.48 \end{array}$$

What if the decimals do not have the same number of digits to the right of the decimal point?

No problem! You can use zeros as place holders.

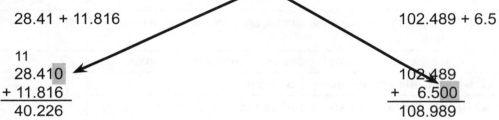

28.41 + 11.816

$$\begin{array}{r} 11 \\ 28.410 \\ +\ 11.816 \\ \hline 40.226 \end{array}$$

102.489 + 6.5

$$\begin{array}{r} 102.489 \\ +\ \ \ 6.500 \\ \hline 108.989 \end{array}$$

Possible Pitfall...

Be sure to line up decimal points before lining up the digits. Find the sum of 82.63 and 4.285.

The RIGHT Way
$$\begin{array}{r} 82.630 \\ +\ \ 4.285 \\ \hline 86.915 \end{array}$$

PITFALL
$$\begin{array}{r} 82.63 \\ +\ \ 4.285 \\ \hline 12.548 \end{array}$$

Show what you know!

Find the sum.

1. 32.5 + 18.3 = _____

2. 115.294 + 4.23 = _____

3. 2.648 + 18.3647 = _____

4. 36.25 + 8.91 = _____

5. 261.478 + 123.21 = _____

6. 4.603 + 9.7 = _____

7. 19.005 + 28.1248 = _____

8. 526.11 + 6.3847 = _____

Name: _____ Date: _____

Unit 1: Decimals

Lesson 2: Subtracting Decimals

Here's the Info...

To subtract decimals, you need to follow the same basic steps that you used when adding decimals. Find the **_difference_** of 35.68 and 14.25.

Step 1: Line up the decimal points.

$$\begin{array}{r} 35.68 \\ -\ 14.25 \\ \hline \end{array}$$

Step 2: Bring down the decimal point.

Step 3: Subtract.

$$\begin{array}{r} 35.68 \\ -\ 14.25 \\ \hline 21.43 \end{array}$$

If the numbers do not have the same number of digits to the right of the decimal point, you can use zeros as place holders. Regroup the same way you would when subtracting whole numbers with zeros. Here are a couple of examples.

$$48.6 - 21.514$$

$$\begin{array}{r} 48.600 \\ -\ 21.514 \\ \hline 27.086 \end{array}$$

$$98.463 - 22.1$$

$$\begin{array}{r} 98.463 \\ -\ 22.100 \\ \hline 76.363 \end{array}$$

Possible Pitfall...

Remember: It is important to line up decimal points first. Do not line up the digits first.

Find the difference of 79.9 and 2.86.

The RIGHT Way

$$\begin{array}{r} 79.90 \\ -\ 2.86 \\ \hline 77.04 \end{array}$$

PITFALL

$$\begin{array}{r} 79.9 \\ -\ 2.86 \\ \hline 5.13 \end{array}$$

Show what you know!

Find the difference.

1. 28.6 – 21.3 = _____

2. 95.413 – 57.29 = _____

3. 129.6 – 28.57 = _____

4. 48.52 – 26.91 = _____

5. 249.587 – 123.14 = _____

6. 8.7 – 6.23 = _____

7. 44.603 – 21.4531 = _____

8. 62.809 – 54.11 = _____

Name: _____ Date: _____

Unit 1: Decimals

Lesson 3: Multiplying Decimals

Here's the Info...

Multiplying decimals is similar to multiplying multi-digit numbers. Let's multiply a decimal by a whole number first. Find the **_product_** of 21.642 and 3.

Step 1:   Write the problem vertically. Write the number with the most digits on top. Unlike adding and subtracting decimals, you don't have to worry about lining up the decimal points.

$$\begin{array}{r} 21.642 \\ \times\quad\ \ 3 \\ \hline \end{array}$$

Step 2:   Multiply as you would with whole numbers.

$$\begin{array}{r} 21.642 \\ \times\quad\ \ 3 \\ \hline 64926 \end{array}$$

Step 3:   Count how many digits there are to the right of the decimal point in the numbers you are multiplying. This is how many digits you should have to the right of the decimal point in your product. Because 21.642 has 3 digits to the right of the decimal point, then your product should also have 3 digits to the right of the decimal point.

$$\begin{array}{r} 21.642 \\ \times\quad\ \ 3 \\ \hline 64.926 \end{array}$$

Now, let's look at multiplying two decimals. Find the product of 21.642 and 3.2.

Step 1:   Write the problem vertically.

$$\begin{array}{r} 21.642 \\ \times\quad 3.2 \\ \hline \end{array}$$

Step 2:   Multiply.

$$\begin{array}{r} 21.642 \\ \times\quad 3.2 \\ \hline 43284 \\ 64926\ \ \\ \hline 692544 \end{array}$$

Step 3:   Count how many digits there are to the right of the decimal point in the numbers you are multiplying. Because 21.642 has 3 digits to the right of the decimal point and 3.2 has 1 digit to the right of the decimal point, there are a total of 4 digits to the right of the decimal point. So, your product should have 4 digits to the right of the decimal point.

$$\begin{array}{r} 21.642 \\ \times\quad 3.2 \\ \hline 69.2544 \end{array}$$

Name: _____ Date: _____

Unit 1: Decimals

Lesson 3: Multiplying Decimals (cont.)

Let's look at one more example. Notice that in this problem, the smaller number is written on top. We write it on top because it has more digits.

$$
\begin{array}{r}
3.0254 \\
\times\ 78.5 \\
\hline
151270 \\
242032 \\
211778 \\
\hline
237.49390
\end{array}
$$

Show what you know!

Place the decimal point in the correct place in the products below.

1. 123.5 × 4.23 = 5 2 2 4 0 5

2. 3.871 × 25 = 9 6 7 7 5

3. 14.29 × 0.539 = 7 7 0 2 3 1

4. 364 × 5.36 = 1 9 5 1 0 4

5. 1.865 × 0.6334 = 1 1 8 1 2 9 1 0

6. 2,465 × 3,554.2 = 8 7 6 1 1 0 3 0

7. 64.211 × 48.53 = 3 1 1 6 1 5 9 8 3

8. 0.9 × 3.821 = 3 4 3 8 9

Find the product.

9.
$$
\begin{array}{r}
58.21 \\
\times\ \ \ 5 \\
\hline
\end{array}
$$

10.
$$
\begin{array}{r}
125.36 \\
\times\ \ 4.1 \\
\hline
\end{array}
$$

11.
$$
\begin{array}{r}
0.2534 \\
\times\ 6.32 \\
\hline
\end{array}
$$

12.
$$
\begin{array}{r}
8,125 \\
\times\ 0.03 \\
\hline
\end{array}
$$

Rewrite each problem vertically. Then, find the product.

13. 61.247 × 2 = _____

14. 13.51 × 3.4 = _____

15. 321.6 × 0.023 = _____

16. 215 × 42.2 = _____

17. 0.2852 × 135.4 = _____

18. 9.003 × 5.47 = _____

Name: _____ Date: _____

Unit 1: Decimals

Lesson 4: Dividing Decimals

Here's the Info...

If you can do long division, you can divide decimals. Let's start by dividing a decimal by a whole number. Find the **_quotient_** of 15.6 and 2.

Step 1:   Write the problem using a long-division symbol.

$$2\overline{)15.6}$$

Step 2:   Move the decimal point in the **_dividend_** up. This is where the decimal point will be in your quotient.

$$2\overline{)15.6}$$

Step 3:   Divide as you would with whole numbers.

$$\begin{array}{r} 7.8 \\ 2\overline{)15.6} \\ -14 \\ \hline 16 \\ -16 \\ \hline 0 \end{array}$$

Now, let's take a look at dividing a decimal by another decimal. The process is similar, but we need to add a couple of steps between Steps 1 and 2 above. Find the quotient of 5.75 and 2.3.

Step 1:   Write the problem using a long-division symbol.

$$2.3\overline{)5.75}$$

Step 2:   Make the **_divisor_** a whole number by moving the decimal point to the right.

$$2.3\overline{)5.75}$$

Step 3:   Move the decimal point in the dividend to the right the same number of places you moved it in the divisor.

$$2.3\overline{)57.5}$$

Step 4:   Move the decimal point up. This is where the decimal point will be in your quotient.

$$23\overline{)57.5}$$

Step 5:   Divide.

$$\begin{array}{r} 2.5 \\ 23\overline{)57.5} \\ -46 \\ \hline 115 \\ -115 \\ \hline 0 \end{array}$$

Math Reference for Middle Grades

Name: _____ Date: _____

Unit 1: Decimals

Lesson 4: Dividing Decimals (cont.)

One more example...

If the dividend does not have as many digits to the right of the decimal point as the divisor, you can use zeros as place holders.

Find the quotient of 11.7 and 2.34.

Because the divisor 2.34 has 2 digits to the right of the decimal point and the dividend 11.7 has only 1, you need a place holder.

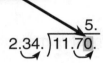

$$2.34. \overline{)11.70.}$$

Show what you know!

Find the quotient.

1. $3 \overline{)11.4}$ 2. $4.2 \overline{)28.14}$ 3. $1.24 \overline{)18.6}$ 4. $2.13 \overline{)18.318}$

5. $49.2 \div 3 =$ _____   6. $100.5 \div 15 =$ _____

7. $187.28 \div 8 =$ _____   8. $68.25 \div 21 =$ _____

9. $52.6 \div 1.6 =$ _____   10. $21.28 \div 3.8 =$ _____

11. $42.194 \div 14.6 =$ _____   12. $107.88 \div 23.2 =$ _____

13. $43.86 \div 2.58 =$ _____   14. $37.177 \div 3.29 =$ _____

15. $53 \div 26.5 =$ _____   16. $58.5 \div 2.25 =$ _____

Name: _____ Date: _____

Unit 2: Pre-Algebra

Lesson 5: Factors and Greatest Common Factor

Here's the Info...

A **_factor_** is a number that divides evenly into a larger number.

6 is a factor of 24 because 24 ÷ 6 = 4.

Some other factors of 24 are 2, 3, 4, and 8. Can you see why?

The **_Greatest Common Factor_** or **_GCF_** of two numbers is the largest number that is a factor of both numbers.

18 and 24 have a GCF of 6 because 6 is the largest number that is a factor of both 18 and 24.

Factors of 18: 1, 2, 3, 6, 9, 18
Factors of 24: 1, 2, 3, 4, 6, 8, 12, 24

Let's see one more example...

Find the GCF of 36 and 54.

Factors of 36: 1, 2, 3, 4, 6, 9, 12, 18, 36
Factors of 54: 1, 2, 3, 6, 9, 18, 27, 54

18 is the Greatest Common Factor of 36 and 54.

Show what you know!

True or False?

1. 5 is a factor of 15 _____   2. 6 is a factor of 16 _____

3. 3 is a factor of 19 _____   4. 7 is a factor of 28 _____

Find the GCF of each pair of numbers.

5. 12 and 28 _____   6. 30 and 45 _____

7. 20 and 35 _____   8. 16 and 40 _____

Name: _____ Date: _____

Unit 2: Pre-Algebra

Lesson 6: Prime Factorization

Here's the Info...

A **_prime number_** is a number whose only **_factors_** are 1 and the number itself.

The first ten prime numbers are 2, 3, 5, 7, 11, 13, 17, 19, 23, and 29.

Finding the prime factors of a number is different from just listing the factors. You must be sure all factors are prime numbers.

To keep it simple, let's use a diagram called a **_factor tree_**.

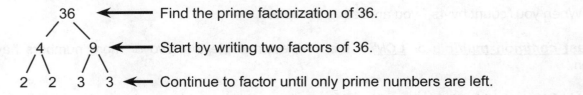

```
       36    ◄──────  Find the prime factorization of 36.
      /  \
     4    9  ◄──────  Start by writing two factors of 36.
    / \  / \
   2  2  3  3  ◄────  Continue to factor until only prime numbers are left.

   2 x 2 x 3 x 3 represents the prime factorization of 36.
```

Possible Pitfall...

The prime factorization does <u>not</u> include every number in the factor tree. Only the prime numbers at the ends or "leaves" of each branch make up the prime factorization.

The RIGHT Way: 2 x 2 x 3 x 3 = 36   **PITFALL:** 4 x 9 x 2 x 2 x 3 x 3 = 1,296

Show what you know!

Find the prime factorization for each number. If the number is prime, answer "Prime."

1. 60 = _____   2. 100 = _____

3. 66 = _____   4. 41 = _____

5. 82 = _____   6. 38 = _____

7. 64 = _____   8. 29 = _____

9. 90 = _____   10. 320 = _____

Name: _____   Date: _____

Unit 2: Pre-Algebra

Lesson 7: Multiples and Least Common Multiple

Here's the Info...

The **_multiples_** of a number are found by multiplying that number by **_counting numbers_**.

> 4 x 1 = **4**
> 4 x 2 = **8**
> 4 x 3 = **12**
> 4 x 4 = **16**

The numbers 4, 8, 12, and 16 are the first four multiples of 4.

When you "count by 4s," you are listing multiples!

The **_least common multiple_** or **_LCM_** is the smallest multiple that two or more numbers have in common.

The LCM of 12 and 15 is 60 because 60 is the smallest number that is a multiple of both 12 and 15.

> **Multiples of 12:** 12, 24, 36, 48, 60, 72, 84, 96, 108, 120,…
> **Multiples of 15:** 15, 30, 45, 60, 75, 90, 105, 120, 135, 150,…

There's another way!

Prime factors can also help us to find the LCM.

Step 1:   List the prime factors of each number.

Step 2:   Line up the like factors in columns.

Step 3:   Bring down <u>one</u> prime factor from each column and multiply.

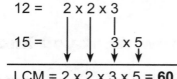

$$12 = 2 \times 2 \times 3$$
$$15 = \qquad\quad 3 \times 5$$
$$LCM = 2 \times 2 \times 3 \times 5 = \mathbf{60}$$

Show what you know!

List the first five multiples of each number.

1. 6: _____   2. 14: _____

Find the LCM of the numbers.

3. 9 and 21: _____   4. 6 and 15: _____   5. 30 and 45: _____

6. 18 and 24: _____   7. 10 and 12: _____   8. 8, 9, and 12: _____

Name: _____   Date: _____

Unit 2: Pre-Algebra

Lesson 8: Exponents and Properties of Exponents

Here's the Info...

__*Exponents*__ are used to show repeated multiplication of a number called the __*base*__.

$2 \times 2 \times 2 \times 2 \times 2 \times 2 \times 2 \times 2 = \mathbf{2^8}$ **Base**^{Exponent}

Exponents are also called __*powers*__ because $\mathbf{2^8}$ is read aloud as *"two to the eighth power."*

Does it work for any number? You bet! Here's an example using 4 as the base.

$4 \times 4 \times 4 \times 4 \times 4 \times 4 \times 4 \times 4 \times 4 = \mathbf{4^9}$ Read *"four to the ninth power"*

Some important properties of exponents are shown in the table below.

Property	Example
Any number (except 0) to the zero power is 1.	$5^0 = 1$
Any number to the first power is equal to itself.	$7^1 = 7$
When multiplying two numbers with the same base, *add* exponents.	$2^3 \times 2^4 = 2^7$
When raising a number with an exponent to a power, *multiply* exponents.	$(3^2)^4 = 3^8$
When raising a __*product*__ to a power, multiply the outer exponent by every inside exponent.	$(8^3 \times 8^2)^4 = 8^{12} \times 8^8 = 8^{20}$

Possible Pitfalls...

When multiplying two numbers with the same base, do <u>not</u> multiply the bases.

The RIGHT Way   **PITFALL**

$5^2 \times 5^6 = \boxed{5^8}$ $5^2 \times 5^6 = 25^8$

The last property in the chart above does <u>not</u> work for sums and differences!!!

The RIGHT Way   **PITFALL**

$(2 + 3)^2 = (5)^2 = 25$ $(2 + 3)^2 = (2^2 + 3^2) = (4 + 9) = 13$

Name: _____   Date: _____

Unit 2: Pre-Algebra

Lesson 8: Exponents and Properties of Exponents (cont.)

Show what you know!

Write using exponents.

1. $4 \times 4 \times 4 \times 4 \times 4 =$ _____

2. $10 \times 10 \times 10 \times 10 \times 10 \times 10 \times 10 =$ _____

3. $3 \times 3 \times 3 \times 6 \times 6 =$ _____

4. $8 \times 8 \times 8 \times 8 \times 5 \times 5 \times 5 \times 5 =$ _____

Use properties of exponents to simplify.

5. $2^0 =$ _____

6. $4^1 =$ _____

7. $9^2 \times 9^6 =$ _____

8. $(5^6)^3 =$ _____

9. $8^2 \times 8^5 =$ _____

10. $(7^3 \times 7^6)^2 =$ _____

11. $(3 + 4)^2 =$ _____

12. $(4^5)^2 =$ _____

Name: _____ Date: _____

 Unit 2: Pre-Algebra

Lesson 9: Order of Operations

Here's the Info...

One *operation* between two numbers is easy enough.　　　$2 \times 5 = 10$

But what happens when there is more than one operation?　　$2 + 5 \times 3 = ?$

Are there two right answers?　　　$7 \times 3 = \boxed{21}?$ **or** $2 + 15 = \boxed{17}?$

The only right answer is 17 because the correct *order of operations* was used.

Here's how it works:

P:	Do all operations in parentheses first.
E:	Apply any *exponents*.
MD:	Do all multiplication and division, working from left to right.
AS:	Do all addition and subtraction, working from left to right.

Remember the letters **P E M D A S** or a sentence like "**P**ink **E**lephants **M**ake **D**andy **A**pple**S**auce." These letters will help you to remember the right order of operations to use.

Possible Pitfall...

Be careful to work multiplication and division *from left to right*.

The RIGHT Way

$12 \div 3 \times 2 =$
　$4 \quad \times 2 =$
　　　8

PITFALL

$12 \div 3 \times 2 =$
$12 \div \quad 6 \quad =$
　　　　2

Show what you know!

Evaluate using the order of operations.

1. $6 + 7 \times 8 =$ _____

2. $16 \div 8 - 2 =$ _____

3. $(25 - 11) \times 3 =$ _____

4. $9 \times 4 - 6 \div 3 =$ _____

5. $16 \div 4 \times 2 =$ _____

6. $2 \times 9 \div 3 =$ _____

7. $9 + 6 \times (8 - 5) =$ _____

8. $(14 - 5) \div (9 - 6) =$ _____

9. $3^2 \times (4 - 2) =$ _____

10. $2 \times (5 + 4) \div 3^2 - 1 =$ _____

Name: _____ Date: _____

Unit 2: Pre-Algebra

Lesson 10: Square Roots and Approximating Square Roots

Here's the Info...

Raising a number to the second power is also known as **_squaring_**.

$3^2 = 3 \times 3 = 9$

The opposite of squaring a number is finding the **_square root_**.

$\sqrt{9} = 3$

What is the square root of 25?

THINK: What number times itself makes 25?
$5 \times 5 = 25$
The square root of 25 is 5 or $\sqrt{25} = 5$.

What if there is not a number times itself that will make the given number?

No problem! We can approximate the square root in two different ways.

TAKE A GUESS

$\sqrt{12} = ?$ How close can you guess?

$3 \times 3 = \boxed{9}$ That's pretty close, but too small.
$4 \times 4 = \boxed{16}$ This one's too big.
Estimate the square root is between 3 and 4.

CALCULATE

$\sqrt{12} = ?$ Grab your calculator!

Find the square root key $\boxed{\sqrt{}}$. You may find it above the $\boxed{x^2}$ key. If so, you will need to press $\boxed{\text{INV}}$ or $\boxed{2^{nd}}$, then $\boxed{\sqrt{}}$.
The approximate square root is 3.464.

Show what you know!

Find each square root.

1. $\sqrt{16} =$ _____   2. $\sqrt{64} =$ _____   3. $\sqrt{100} =$ _____   4. $\sqrt{81} =$ _____

Estimate each square root without a calculator.

5. $\sqrt{21} =$ _____   6. $\sqrt{65} =$ _____   7. $\sqrt{104} =$ _____   8. $\sqrt{7} =$ _____

Estimate each square root using a calculator and round to the nearest thousandths.

9. $\sqrt{21} =$ _____   10. $\sqrt{65} =$ _____   11. $\sqrt{104} =$ _____   12. $\sqrt{7} =$ _____

Name: _____ Date: _____

  Unit 2: Pre-Algebra

Lesson 11: Scientific Notation

Here's the Info...

**Scientific notation** is used to make it easier to work with very large and very small numbers.

Changing to scientific notation:

Step 1:	Move the decimal to make a number between 1 and 10.	250,000.
Step 2:	Count the decimal places the decimal point moved.	2.50000
		5 decimal places
Step 3:	Write the number without the extra zeros and multiply by a _**power**_ of 10. (This is also known as the exponent.) The power tells how many places the decimal point was moved.	2.5×10^5

What if the number is very small?

Move the decimal point to the RIGHT to make a number between 1 and 10, and then use a NEGATIVE power of 10.

0.0000046
6 places
4.6×10^{-6}

Changing to standard form:

Step 1:	Since the exponent is positive, make a LARGE number.	5.3×10^7
Step 2:	Move the decimal point to the RIGHT the number of times shown by the _**exponent**_. Add extra zeros to fill in the spaces.	5.3000000
		7 places
Step 3:	Write the number in standard form.	53,000,000

Show what you know!

Write each number in scientific notation.

1. 73,000 = _____
2. 62,000,000 = _____
3. 821,000 = _____

4. 0.000037 = _____
5. 0.00039 = _____
6. 0.0000007 = _____

Write each number in standard form.

7. 2.4×10^5 = _____
8. 4.9×10^7 = _____
9. 7.43×10^4 = _____

10. 4.9×10^{-6} = _____
11. 2.03×10^{-3} = _____
12. 8×10^{-5} = _____

Name: _____ Date: _____

Unit 2: Pre-Algebra

Lesson 12: Variables and Evaluating Expressions

Here's the Info...

A **_variable_** is a symbol (usually a letter) that stands for an unknown number.

A **_term_** is a number, variable, or a number and a variable combined with multiplication or division.

An **_expression_** is a term or collection of terms separated by addition or subtraction.

Expression	Number of Terms	Variables Used
$4z$	One	z
$5x - 3$	Two	x
$6y + 4a - 2$	Three	y, a
$2L + 2W$	Two	L, W

Does the last expression look familiar? That's the formula for the **_perimeter_** of a rectangle.

To **_evaluate_** an expression, follow these steps: $2L + 2W$ where $L = 6$ and $W = 2$

Step 1:   Substitute numbers in place of each variable. $2(6) + 2(2)$

Step 2:   Use order of operations to simplify. $12 \ + \ 4 = 16$

Possible Pitfall...

Use parentheses and be sure to follow the order of operations carefully.

The RIGHT Way

a^2b where $a = -2$ and $b = 3$
$(-2)^2(3)$
   $4(3)$
   12

PITFALL

a^2b where $a = -2$ and $b = 3$
$-2^2(3)$
$-4(3)$
-12

Show what you know!

Evaluate each expression for $x = 2$, $y = -3$, and $z = 5$.

1. $6x - 11 =$ _____

2. $z - y =$ _____

3. $xyz =$ _____

4. $(z + y) \div x =$ _____

5. $4y + 5 + y^2 =$ _____

6. $8y \div x =$ _____

Name: _____ Date: _____

Unit 2: Pre-Algebra

Lesson 13: Simplifying Expressions

Here's the Info...

Like terms contain the same **variable** with the same **exponent**.

     Like Terms: $3x$ and $5x$ Not Like Terms: $8x$ and 10

Expressions are simplified when all of the like terms have been combined.

To combine like terms, add the numbers in front of the variables (called **coefficients**).

     $3x + 5x = (3 + 5)x = 8x$

Possible Pitfall...

When combining like terms, do not change the power of the variable.

    The RIGHT Way   **PITFALL**

    $2c + 7c = 9c$ $2c + 7c = 9c^2$

It is also helpful to know how to write an expression without parentheses.

Use the **Distributive Property**! $2(3x + 5)$

Step 1:   Multiply the **factor** of 2 by each term inside the parentheses. $(2 \cdot 3x) + (2 \cdot 5)$

Step 2:   Simplify carefully using the **order of operations**. $6x + 10$

Show what you know!

Simplify each expression.

1. $4z + 2z =$ _____   2. $2x + 5x =$ _____   3. $8y + 4y + y =$ _____

4. $3a - 5a =$ _____   5. $4b + 5a - b =$ _____   6. $6(3k + 2k) =$ _____

7. $x + 4(3x + 5) =$ _____   8. $4(w + 2x) + 9w =$ _____

9. $2(4n + 3) + 8 =$ _____   10. $5(-7x + 1) - 5 =$ _____

11. $3m + 2(6m + 5) + 8 =$ _____   12. $7(2a + b) + 8(3 + b) =$ _____

Name: _____   Date: _____

Unit 3: Fractions and Mixed Numbers

Lesson 14: Equivalent Fractions

Here's the Info...

Equivalent fractions are different fractions that name the same amount.

This fraction bar represents the fraction $\frac{1}{2}$, because it has been divided into 2 equal parts and 1 of them is shaded.

This fraction bar represents the fraction $\frac{3}{6}$, because it has been divided into 6 equal parts and 3 of them are shaded. Notice how the 3 shaded parts of this fraction bar are equal to the 1 shaded part of the fraction bar above.

From these fraction bars, we can see that $\frac{1}{2}$ and $\frac{3}{6}$ are equivalent fractions.

We can find many other equivalent fractions for $\frac{1}{2}$ by multiplying the ***numerator*** and ***denominator*** by the same number.

$$\frac{1 \times 2}{2 \times 2} = \frac{2}{4} \qquad\qquad \frac{1 \times 6}{2 \times 6} = \frac{6}{12} \qquad\qquad \frac{1 \times 15}{2 \times 15} = \frac{15}{30}$$

Therefore, $\frac{2}{4}$, $\frac{6}{12}$, and $\frac{15}{30}$ are all equivalent to $\frac{1}{2}$.

We can also find equivalent fractions by dividing the numerator and denominator of a fraction by the same number. Let's find a fraction that is equivalent to $\frac{16}{20}$. $\qquad \frac{16 \div 4}{20 \div 4} = \frac{4}{5}$

Therefore, we can say that $\frac{4}{5}$ is equivalent to $\frac{16}{20}$.

Show what you know!

Write two equivalent fractions for each of the given fractions.

1. $\frac{2}{3}$ _____   2. $\frac{14}{21}$ _____   3. $\frac{3}{4}$ _____

4. $\frac{36}{48}$ _____   5. $\frac{5}{8}$ _____   6. $\frac{72}{100}$ _____

Name: _____

Date: _____

Unit 3: Fractions and Mixed Numbers

Lesson 15: Simplest Form

Here's the Info...

When you are asked to write a fraction in **_simplest form_**, you are looking for an **_equivalent fraction_**. More specifically, you are looking for the fraction that is equivalent to your given fraction and whose **_numerator_** and **_denominator_** has a **_Greatest Common Factor (GCF)_** of 1.

Write $\frac{24}{32}$ in simplest form.

Step 1: Determine the GCF of the numerator and denominator.

24: 1, 2, 3, 4, 6, ⑧ 12, 24
32: 1, 2, 4, ⑧ 16, 32

Step 2: Divide the numerator and denominator by the GCF.

$$\frac{24 \div 8}{32 \div 8} = \frac{3}{4}$$

Step 3: Check to make sure that 1 is now the GCF of the numerator and denominator.

3: ① 3
4: ① 2, 4

Therefore, $\frac{3}{4}$ is the simplest form of $\frac{24}{32}$.

Possible Pitfall...

Be sure to divide the numerator and denominator of the fraction you are trying to simplify by the GCF. If you divide it by a factor that is not the GCF, you will not be finding the simplest form.

For example, we can divide the numerator and denominator of $\frac{24}{32}$ by 4 and get $\frac{6}{8}$. However, the GCF of 6 and 8 is not 1, so we know that it is not in simplest form!

Show what you know!

Write each fraction in simplest form.

1. $\frac{48}{60}$ = _____

2. $\frac{25}{45}$ = _____

3. $\frac{8}{12}$ = _____

4. $\frac{8}{15}$ = _____

5. $\frac{26}{39}$ = _____

6. $\frac{15}{40}$ = _____

7. $\frac{72}{81}$ = _____

8. $\frac{70}{84}$ = _____

9. $\frac{52}{60}$ = _____

Name: _____   Date: _____

Unit 3: Fractions and Mixed Numbers

Lesson 16: Adding and Subtracting Fractions With Like Denominators

Here's the Info...

Adding and subtracting fractions can be easy when the **_denominators_** are the same.

Find the **_sum_** of $\frac{2}{9}$ and $\frac{4}{9}$.

Step 1: The fractions have the same denominator. So, add the **_numerators_**, and write their sum over the denominator.

$$\frac{2}{⑨} + \frac{4}{⑨} = \frac{2+4}{9} = \frac{6}{9}$$

Step 2: Write the answer in **_simplest form_**.

$$\frac{2}{9} + \frac{4}{9} = \frac{6}{9} = \frac{2}{3}$$

Follow these same steps when subtracting fractions with like denominators. Here's an example.

$$\frac{11}{12} - \frac{5}{12} = \frac{6}{12} = \frac{1}{2}$$

Possible Pitfall...

NEVER add or subtract the denominators.

The RIGHT Way

$$\frac{2}{15} + \frac{4}{15} = \frac{6}{15} = \frac{2}{5}$$

PITFALL

$$\frac{2}{15} + \frac{4}{15} = \frac{6}{30} = \frac{1}{5}$$

Show what you know!

Find the sum or difference as indicated. Write your answer in simplest form.

1. $\frac{1}{5} + \frac{2}{5}$ = _____

2. $\frac{3}{7} + \frac{2}{7}$ = _____

3. $\frac{1}{4} + \frac{1}{4}$ = _____

4. $\frac{4}{11} + \frac{5}{11}$ = _____

5. $\frac{8}{9} - \frac{5}{9}$ = _____

6. $\frac{6}{7} - \frac{2}{7}$ = _____

7. $\frac{9}{10} - \frac{3}{10}$ = _____

8. $\frac{11}{12} - \frac{7}{12}$ = _____

Name: _____ Date: _____

Unit 3: Fractions and Mixed Numbers

Lesson 17: Adding and Subtracting Mixed Numbers With Like Denominators and No Regrouping

Here's the Info...

The process for adding and subtracting mixed numbers with **_like_** **_denominators_** is similar to the process for adding and subtracting fractions with like denominators.

Find the **_sum_** of $4\frac{1}{8}$ and $2\frac{3}{8}$.

Step 1: Write the problem horizontally.

$$4\frac{1}{8} + 2\frac{3}{8}$$

Step 2: Because the fractional parts of the mixed numbers have the same denominator, you can add the **_numerators_** and write their sum over the denominator.

$$\frac{1}{⑧} + \frac{3}{⑧} = \frac{1+3}{8} = \frac{4}{8}$$

Step 3: Now, add the whole numbers.

$$4\frac{1}{8} + 2\frac{3}{8} = 6\frac{4}{8}$$

Step 4: Write the answer in **_simplest form_**.

$$4\frac{1}{8} + 2\frac{3}{8} = 6\frac{1}{2}$$

Follow these same steps when subtracting mixed numbers with like denominators. Here is an example.

$$3\frac{5}{6} - 1\frac{1}{6} = 2\frac{4}{6} = 2\frac{2}{3}$$

Possible Pitfall...

NEVER add or subtract the denominators.

The RIGHT Way

$$5\frac{5}{18} + 1\frac{7}{18} = 6\frac{12}{18} = 6\frac{2}{3}$$

PITFALL

$$5\frac{5}{18} + 1\frac{7}{18} = 6\frac{12}{36} = 6\frac{1}{3}$$

Show what you know!

Find the sum or difference as indicated. Write your answer in simplest form.

1. $2\frac{1}{3} + 5\frac{1}{3} =$ _____

2. $4\frac{3}{14} + 6\frac{5}{14} =$ _____

3. $3\frac{1}{8} + 9\frac{1}{8} =$ _____

4. $8\frac{2}{13} + 3\frac{6}{13} =$ _____

5. $6\frac{17}{18} - 1\frac{5}{18} =$ _____

6. $5\frac{9}{14} - 3\frac{3}{14} =$ _____

7. $8\frac{8}{11} - 2\frac{5}{11} =$ _____

8. $9\frac{3}{5} - 4\frac{2}{5} =$ _____

Name: _____ Date: _____

Unit 3: Fractions and Mixed Numbers

Lesson 18: Adding and Subtracting Fractions With Unlike Denominators

Here's the Info...

Let's take a look at adding and subtracting fractions with unlike denominators.

Find the **_sum_** of $\frac{1}{4}$ and $\frac{3}{8}$.

Step 1: Find a **_common denominator_**. A common denominator is a **_multiple_** of the denominators. Usually the **_least common multiple_** (LCM) is used. The LCM is 8. So, it becomes the **_least common denominator_** (LCD).

4: 4, ⑧ 12, 16, 20
8: ⑧ 16, 24, 32, 40

Step 2: Write an **_equivalent fraction_** for $\frac{1}{4}$ with the LCD.

$\frac{1}{4} = \frac{1 \times 2}{4 \times 2} = \frac{2}{8}$

$\frac{3}{8}$ is already written with the LCD.

Step 3: Add the numerators and write their sum over the LCD.

$\frac{2}{8} + \frac{3}{8} = \frac{5}{8}$

Step 4: Write your answer in **_simplest form_**.

$\frac{1}{4} + \frac{3}{8} = \frac{5}{8}$

Follow these same steps when subtracting fractions with unlike denominators. Here is an example.

$$\frac{8}{9} - \frac{1}{4} = \frac{32}{36} - \frac{9}{36} = \frac{23}{36}$$

Possible Pitfall...

You must find a common denominator before adding or subtracting. Do NOT add or subtract denominators.

The RIGHT Way

$\frac{2}{5} + \frac{1}{3} = \frac{6}{15} + \frac{5}{15} = \frac{11}{15}$

PITFALL

$\frac{2}{5} + \frac{1}{3} = \frac{3}{8}$

Show what you know!

Find the sum or difference. Write your answer in simplest form.

1. $\frac{2}{5} + \frac{3}{10} =$ _____

2. $\frac{4}{9} + \frac{1}{3} =$ _____

3. $\frac{3}{16} + \frac{5}{24} =$ _____

4. $\frac{1}{6} + \frac{1}{4} =$ _____

5. $\frac{9}{10} - \frac{2}{5} =$ _____

6. $\frac{7}{8} - \frac{5}{24} =$ _____

7. $\frac{3}{4} - \frac{1}{3} =$ _____

8. $\frac{4}{5} - \frac{1}{7} =$ _____

Name: ______________________________ Date: ______________

Unit 3: Fractions and Mixed Numbers

Lesson 19: Adding and Subtracting Mixed Numbers With Unlike Denominators and No Regrouping

Here's the Info...

Let's add and subtract mixed numbers with unlike denominators.

Find the ***sum*** of $2\frac{3}{7}$ and $1\frac{4}{21}$.

Step 1: Find the ***least common denominator*** (LCD) for the fractional parts of the mixed numbers. The ***LCM*** of 7 and 21 is 21. So, 21 is the LCD.

7: 7, 14, (21), 28, 35, 42
21: (21), 42, 63, 84, 105

Step 2: Write an ***equivalent fraction*** for $\frac{3}{7}$ with the LCD.

$\frac{4}{21}$ is already written with the LCD.

$$\frac{3}{7} = \frac{3 \times 3}{7 \times 3} = \frac{9}{21}$$

Step 3: Add the numerators and write their sum over the LCD.

$$\frac{9}{21} + \frac{4}{21} = \frac{13}{21}$$

Step 4: Add the whole numbers.

Step 5: Write your answer in ***simplest form***.

$$2\frac{3}{7} + 1\frac{4}{21} = 3\frac{13}{21}$$

Follow these steps when subtracting mixed numbers with unlike denominators. Here is an example.

$$8\frac{17}{24} - 2\frac{5}{18} = 8\frac{51}{72} - 2\frac{20}{72} = 6\frac{31}{72}$$

Possible Pitfall...

You must find a common denominator before adding or subtracting.
Do NOT add or subtract denominators.

The RIGHT Way

$$10\frac{7}{18} + 3\frac{1}{9} = 13\frac{9}{18} = 13\frac{1}{2}$$

PITFALL

$$10\frac{7}{18} + 3\frac{1}{9} = 13\frac{8}{27}$$

Show what you know!

Find the sum or difference as indicated. Write your answer in simplest form.

1. $6\frac{3}{10} + 2\frac{3}{20}$ = ______________
2. $5\frac{3}{8} + 1\frac{5}{12}$ = ______________
3. $3\frac{1}{8} + 9\frac{5}{8}$ = ______________
4. $4\frac{1}{3} + 9\frac{2}{5}$ = ______________
5. $12\frac{3}{4} - 2\frac{1}{2}$ = ______________
6. $9\frac{2}{3} - 1\frac{1}{6}$ = ______________
7. $6\frac{4}{5} - 5\frac{1}{2}$ = ______________
8. $7\frac{17}{18} - 4\frac{3}{4}$ = ______________

Name: _____ Date: _____

Unit 3: Fractions and Mixed Numbers

Lesson 20: Multiplying Fractions

Here's the Info...

If you know how to add and subtract fractions, multiplying fractions will seem easy! You don't even have to find a common denominator!

Find the **_product_** of $\frac{3}{5}$ and $\frac{7}{9}$.

Step 1: Write the problem horizontally.

$$\frac{3}{5} \times \frac{7}{9}$$

Step 2: Multiply the **_numerators_** and write their product over the product of the **_denominators_**.

$$\frac{3}{5} \times \frac{7}{9} = \frac{3 \times 7}{5 \times 9} = \frac{21}{45}$$

Step 3: Write your answer in **_simplest form_**.

$$\frac{3}{5} \times \frac{7}{9} = \frac{7}{15}$$

Let's look at a couple more examples to make sure you've got it.

Example 1

$$\frac{5}{8} \times \frac{2}{3} = \frac{5 \times 2}{8 \times 3} = \frac{10}{24} = \frac{5}{12}$$

Example 2

$$\frac{7}{12} \times \frac{3}{7} = \frac{7 \times 3}{12 \times 7} = \frac{21}{84} = \frac{1}{4}$$

Show what you know!

Find the product. Write your answer in simplest form.

1. $\frac{3}{5} \times \frac{5}{8}$ = _____

2. $\frac{3}{4} \times \frac{5}{6}$ = _____

3. $\frac{5}{14} \times \frac{7}{9}$ = _____

4. $\frac{9}{11} \times \frac{1}{6}$ = _____

5. $\frac{2}{3} \times \frac{9}{16}$ = _____

6. $\frac{2}{7} \times \frac{8}{9}$ = _____

7. $\frac{8}{25} \times \frac{1}{2}$ = _____

8. $\frac{7}{10} \times \frac{5}{14}$ = _____

Name: _____ Date: _____

Unit 3: Fractions and Mixed Numbers

Lesson 21: Dividing Fractions

Here's the Info...

It may sound strange, but dividing fractions is similar to multiplying fractions. There's just one extra step at the beginning of the process.

Find the **_quotient_** of $\frac{2}{9}$ and $\frac{5}{6}$.

Step 1: Write the problem horizontally. $\frac{2}{9} \div \frac{5}{6}$

Step 2: Invert, or write the **_reciprocal_** of, the second fraction and change the division symbol to a multiplication symbol. $\frac{2}{9} \div \frac{5}{6} = \frac{2}{9} \times \frac{6}{5}$

Step 3: Multiply the **_numerators_** and write their **_product_** over the product of the **_denominators_**. $\frac{2 \times 6}{9 \times 5} = \frac{12}{45}$

Step 4: Write your answer in **_simplest form_**. $\frac{2}{9} \div \frac{5}{6} = \frac{4}{15}$

Take a look at a couple more examples.

Example 1

$\frac{3}{8} \div \frac{3}{4} = \frac{3}{8} \times \frac{4}{3} = \frac{12}{24} = \frac{1}{2}$

Example 2

$\frac{5}{12} \div \frac{10}{11} = \frac{5}{12} \times \frac{11}{10} = \frac{55}{120} = \frac{11}{24}$

Show what you know!

Find the quotient. Write your answer in simplest form.

1. $\frac{5}{8} \div \frac{3}{4}$ = _____

2. $\frac{5}{14} \div \frac{1}{2}$ = _____

3. $\frac{2}{3} \div \frac{14}{15}$ = _____

4. $\frac{6}{13} \div \frac{3}{5}$ = _____

5. $\frac{6}{11} \div \frac{4}{5}$ = _____

6. $\frac{1}{3} \div \frac{17}{18}$ = _____

7. $\frac{3}{8} \div \frac{15}{16}$ = _____

8. $\frac{5}{9} \div \frac{10}{11}$ = _____

Name: _____ Date: _____

Unit 3: Fractions and Mixed Numbers

Lesson 22: Improper Fractions and Mixed Numbers

Here's the Info...

An **_improper fraction_** is a fraction in which the **_numerator_** is greater than the **_denominator_**. You can rewrite improper fractions as mixed numbers. Let's rewrite the improper fraction $\frac{25}{7}$ as a mixed number.

Step 1: The **_fraction bar_** in a fraction indicates division. So, divide the numerator by the denominator. The number of times the denominator divides evenly into the numerator is the whole number of your mixed number.

$$7\overline{)25} \quad \begin{array}{r} ③ \\ -21 \\ \hline ④ \end{array}$$

Step 2: The **_remainder_** is the numerator of the fractional part of the mixed number. It should be written over the original denominator.

$$\frac{25}{7} = 3\frac{4}{7}$$

You use multiplication and addition to convert a mixed number to an improper fraction.

Rewrite $5\frac{2}{9}$ as an improper fraction.

Step 1: Multiply the whole number by the denominator. $5 \times 9 = 45$

Step 2: Add the product from Step 1 to the numerator. $45 + 2 = 47$

Step 3: The result from Step 2 is the numerator of the improper fraction and should be written over the original denominator. $5\frac{2}{9} = \frac{47}{9}$

Show what you know!

Rewrite each improper fraction as a mixed number.

1. $\frac{18}{5}$ = _____   2. $\frac{27}{4}$ = _____   3. $\frac{33}{8}$ = _____   4. $\frac{53}{6}$ = _____

Rewrite each mixed number as an improper fraction.

5. $2\frac{1}{3}$ = _____   6. $4\frac{3}{8}$ = _____   7. $3\frac{5}{16}$ = _____   8. $10\frac{11}{12}$ = _____

Name: _____ Date: _____

Unit 3: Fractions and Mixed Numbers

Lesson 23: Adding Mixed Numbers With Regrouping

Here's the Info...

Sometimes when you are adding mixed numbers, you have to regroup.

Find the **_sum_** of $1\frac{7}{9}$ and $6\frac{5}{9}$.

Step 1: Write the problem horizontally.

$1\frac{7}{9} + 6\frac{5}{9}$

Step 2: Add the whole number parts and the fractional parts. Because the **_denominator_** of both fractions is 9, you do not need to find a **_common denominator_**.

$1\frac{7}{9} + 6\frac{5}{9} = 7\frac{12}{9}$

Step 3: Notice that the fractional part of the mixed number is an **_improper fraction_**. Convert this improper fraction to a mixed number.

$\frac{12}{9} = 1\frac{3}{9}$

Step 4: Add the whole number from Step 3 to the whole number sum in Step 2.

$7 + 1\frac{3}{9} = 8\frac{3}{9}$

Step 5: Write your answer in **_simplest form_**.

$1\frac{7}{9} + 6\frac{5}{9} = 8\frac{1}{3}$

Let's look at an example where you have to find a common denominator *and* regroup.

$4\frac{3}{8} + 2\frac{3}{4} = 4\frac{3}{8} + 2\frac{6}{8} = 6\frac{9}{8} = 7\frac{1}{8}$

Show what you know!

Find the sum. Write your answer in simplest form.

1. $2\frac{4}{5} + 6\frac{3}{5} =$ _____

2. $6\frac{2}{7} + 3\frac{6}{7} =$ _____

3. $3\frac{4}{9} + 2\frac{8}{9} =$ _____

4. $4\frac{2}{3} + 3\frac{5}{9} =$ _____

5. $4\frac{9}{16} + 1\frac{7}{12} =$ _____

6. $1\frac{7}{8} + 2\frac{17}{18} =$ _____

Name: _____ Date: _____

Unit 3: Fractions and Mixed Numbers

Lesson 24: Subtracting Mixed Numbers With Regrouping

Here's the Info...

Sometimes, you'll find that you need to regroup when you are subtracting mixed numbers. Here's how you do it.

Find the **_difference_** of $4\frac{1}{6}$ and $2\frac{5}{6}$.

Step 1:   Write the problem horizontally.

$$4\frac{1}{6} - 2\frac{5}{6}$$

Step 2:   You need to subtract the fractional parts, but $\frac{1}{6}$ is less than $\frac{5}{6}$. So, you must regroup. Borrow 1 from the 4 in $4\frac{1}{6}$, and rewrite it as $\frac{6}{6}$, so that we can add it to $\frac{1}{6}$.

$$1 = \frac{6}{6}$$

$$\frac{6}{6} + \frac{1}{6} = \frac{7}{6}$$

$$4\frac{1}{6} = 3\frac{7}{6}$$

Step 3:   Subtract the whole number parts and the fractional parts. Because the **_denominator_** of both fractions is 6, you do not need to find a **_common denominator_**.

$$4\frac{1}{6} - 2\frac{5}{6} = 3\frac{7}{6} - 2\frac{5}{6}$$

Step 4:   Write your answer in **_simplest form_**.

$$= 1\frac{2}{6} = 1\frac{1}{3}$$

Let's look at an example where you have to find a common denominator *and* regroup.

$$8\frac{2}{3} - 5\frac{14}{15} = 8\frac{10}{15} - 5\frac{14}{15} = 7\frac{25}{15} - 5\frac{14}{15} = 2\frac{11}{15}$$

Show what you know!

Find the sum. Write your answer in simplest form.

1. $8\frac{1}{3} - 5\frac{2}{3} =$ _____

2. $5\frac{3}{8} - 1\frac{7}{8} =$ _____

3. $9\frac{2}{5} - 2\frac{4}{5} =$ _____

4. $5\frac{1}{20} - 2\frac{9}{10} =$ _____

5. $6\frac{3}{8} - 4\frac{7}{12} =$ _____

6. $10\frac{1}{6} - 6\frac{7}{9} =$ _____

Name: _____ Date: _____

Unit 3: Fractions and Mixed Numbers

Lesson 25: Multiplying Mixed Numbers

Here's the Info...

If you know how to multiply fractions and rewrite mixed numbers as **_improper fractions_**, then you have the skills you need to multiply mixed numbers.

Let's look at an example. Find the **_product_** of $2\frac{3}{4}$ and $1\frac{2}{3}$.

Step 1: Write the problem horizontally.

$$2\frac{3}{4} \times 1\frac{2}{3}$$

Step 2: Rewrite the mixed numbers as improper fractions.

$$2\frac{3}{4} \times 1\frac{2}{3} = \frac{11}{4} \times \frac{5}{3}$$

Step 3: Multiply the **_numerators_** and write their product over the product of the denominators.

$$\frac{11}{4} \times \frac{5}{3} = \frac{55}{12}$$

Step 4: Write your answer in **_simplest form_**. When your answer is an improper fraction, it is best to rewrite it as a mixed number. Leaving it as an improper fraction just wouldn't be proper!

$$2\frac{3}{4} \times 1\frac{2}{3} = 4\frac{7}{12}$$

Let's look at one more example.

$$2\frac{1}{9} \times 3\frac{1}{5} = \frac{19}{9} \times \frac{16}{5} = \frac{304}{45} = 6\frac{34}{45}$$

Show what you know!

Find the product. Write your answer as a mixed number in simplest form.

1. $3\frac{2}{3} \times 4\frac{1}{8} =$ _____

2. $3\frac{3}{4} \times 2\frac{6}{7} =$ _____

3. $1\frac{5}{6} \times 5\frac{1}{4} =$ _____

4. $6\frac{2}{5} \times 2\frac{4}{7} =$ _____

5. $8\frac{1}{2} \times 2\frac{1}{6} =$ _____

6. $7\frac{4}{9} \times 3\frac{2}{7} =$ _____

Name: _____ Date: _____

Unit 3: Fractions and Mixed Numbers

Lesson 26: Dividing Mixed Numbers

Here's the Info...

The process for dividing mixed numbers is similar to the process for dividing fractions. There's just one extra step. Take a look.

Find the **_quotient_** of $3\frac{2}{5}$ and $2\frac{1}{4}$.

Step 1: Write the problem horizontally.

$$3\frac{2}{5} \div 2\frac{1}{4}$$

Step 2: Rewrite the mixed numbers as **_improper fractions_**.

$$3\frac{2}{5} \div 2\frac{1}{4} = \frac{17}{5} \div \frac{9}{4}$$

Step 3: Invert, or write the **_reciprocal_** of, the second fraction and change the division symbol to a multiplication symbol.

$$\frac{17}{5} \div \frac{9}{4} = \frac{17}{5} \times \frac{4}{9}$$

Step 4: Multiply the **_numerators_** and write their product over the product of the denominators.

$$\frac{17}{5} \times \frac{4}{9} = \frac{68}{45}$$

Step 5: Write your answer in **_simplest form_**. When your answer is an improper fraction, it is best to rewrite it as a mixed number. Leaving it as an improper fraction just wouldn't be proper!

$$3\frac{2}{5} \div 2\frac{1}{4} = 1\frac{23}{45}$$

Let's look at one more example.

$$1\frac{6}{7} \div 2\frac{3}{4} = \frac{13}{7} \div \frac{11}{4} = \frac{13}{7} \times \frac{4}{11} = \frac{52}{77}$$

Show what you know!

Find the quotient. Write your answer in simplest form.

1. $5\frac{1}{4} \div 3\frac{1}{3}$ = _____

2. $7\frac{5}{6} \div 9\frac{1}{2}$ = _____

3. $3\frac{5}{7} \div 2\frac{1}{2}$ = _____

4. $1\frac{9}{10} \div 5\frac{1}{6}$ = _____

5. $4\frac{5}{9} \div 9\frac{1}{3}$ = _____

6. $8\frac{1}{8} \div 2\frac{6}{7}$ = _____

Name: _____   Date: _____

Unit 4: Ratio, Proportion, and Percents

Lesson 27: Ratio and Proportion

Here's the Info...

A **_ratio_** is a comparison of two numbers.

If a basketball team has 15 wins and 10 losses, then the ratio of *wins to losses* is 15 to 10.

A ratio can be written in three different forms.   15 to 10   15:10 $\frac{15}{10}$

Possible Pitfall...

Always write a ratio of two numbers in the order they are given in the problem. Changing the order will change the ratio.

The RIGHT Way
Wins to losses

15:10 or $\frac{15}{10}$ = $\boxed{\frac{3}{2}}$

PITFALL
Losses to wins

10:15 or $\frac{10}{15}$ = $\boxed{\frac{2}{3}}$

When two ratios are equal, they form a **_proportion_**. A proportion has **_cross products_** that are equal.

$\frac{6}{9}$ = $\frac{8}{12}$ ⟶ Do these two ratios create a proportion?

$\frac{6}{9}$ ⤫ $\frac{8}{12}$ ⟶ Are the cross products equal?

6 x 12 = 8 x 9

72 = 72 ⟶ Yes, $\frac{6}{9}$ = $\frac{8}{12}$ is a proportion.

Show what you know!
A class has 14 boys and 12 girls. Write each ratio.

1. number of boys to girls = _____   2. number of girls to boys = _____

3. number of boys to students = _____   4. number of students to girls = _____

Write = or ≠ in each box to tell whether each pair of ratios forms a proportion.

5. $\frac{4}{7}$ ☐ $\frac{20}{35}$ 6. $\frac{3}{2}$ ☐ $\frac{16}{10}$ 7. $\frac{3}{8}$ ☐ $\frac{16}{42}$ 8. $\frac{10}{4}$ ☐ $\frac{25}{10}$

Name: _____ Date: _____

Unit 4: Ratio, Proportion, and Percents

Lesson 28: Solving Proportions

Here's the Info...

Proportions can be used to solve many types of problems.

Suppose you can buy 5 cookies for $1.20. How much would it cost to buy 12 cookies?

Step 1: Write a proportion that relates two ratios. ⟶ $\dfrac{5 \text{ cookies}}{\$1.20} = \dfrac{12 \text{ cookies}}{x}$

Step 2: Find the **_cross products_**. ⟶ $\dfrac{5}{1.20} \diagup\!\!\!\!\diagdown \dfrac{12}{x}$

$$5x = 12 \cdot 1.20$$

Step 3: Solve the equation by dividing both sides by 5. ⟶ $\dfrac{5x}{5} = \dfrac{14.40}{5}$

$$x = \$2.88$$

Possible Pitfall...

Be sure to express each number in the same units before solving proportions.

An international phone call costs $3.30 for 15 minutes. How much would a 2-hour phone call cost?

The RIGHT Way

$$\frac{\$3.30}{15 \text{ minutes}} = \frac{x}{120 \text{ minutes}}$$

$$3.30 \cdot 120 = 15x$$
$$396 = 15x$$
$$\boxed{\$26.40 = x}$$

PITFALL

$$\frac{\$3.30}{15 \text{ minutes}} = \frac{x}{2 \text{ hours}}$$

$$3.30 \cdot 2 = 15x$$
$$6.60 = 15x$$
$$\boxed{\$0.44 = x}$$

Name: _____ Date: _____

Unit 4: Ratio, Proportion, and Percents

Lesson 28: Solving Proportions (cont.)

Show what you know!

Solve each proportion using cross products.

1. $\dfrac{4}{3} = \dfrac{x}{21}$

2. $\dfrac{13}{a} = \dfrac{39}{60}$

3. $\dfrac{3}{6} = \dfrac{7}{b}$

_____ _____ _____

4. $\dfrac{8}{6} = \dfrac{y}{24}$

5. $\dfrac{w}{9} = \dfrac{8}{3}$

_____ _____

Write a proportion to describe each situation. Then solve.

6. 20 oz. of juice costs $2.50. How much does 32 oz. cost? _____

7. Jack can run 50 yd. in 5 seconds. How far can he run in 8 seconds? _____

8. A lion's heart beats 6 times in 8 seconds. How many times will it beat in 60 seconds?

_____

9. 30 copies cost $3.60. How much will 50 copies cost? _____

10. A car gets 24 miles to one gallon of gas. How much gas will it need to go 120 miles?

_____

Name: _____   Date: _____

Unit 4: Ratio, Proportion, and Percents

Lesson 29: Similar Figures and Scale Factor

Here's the Info...

Similar figures have the same *shape*, but are not necessarily the same *size*.

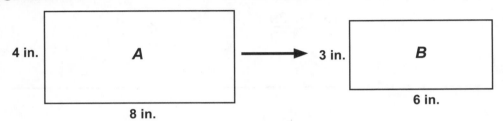

Follow these steps to decide if two figures are similar.

Step 1:   Set up ratios of **_corresponding sides_**. $\dfrac{\text{Length of A}}{\text{Length of B}} = \dfrac{\text{Width of A}}{\text{Width of B}}$ ➡ $\dfrac{8}{6} = \dfrac{4}{3}$

Step 2:   Find **_cross products_** to see if the ratios are equal. $8 \cdot 3 = 4 \cdot 6$

Step 3:   If the sides have equal ratios, the figures are similar. $24 = 24$ ☑

Corresponding sides of similar figures have a common ratio called the **_scale factor_**.

In the rectangles above, the scale factor is $\dfrac{4}{3}$.

All other ratios of corresponding sides will *reduce* to this same ratio. $\dfrac{8 \div 2}{6 \div 2} = \dfrac{4}{3}$

Show what you know!

Determine if the figures are similar. If they are, find the scale factor.

1. Similar? _____   Scale factor: _____

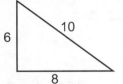

2. Similar? _____   Scale factor: _____

3. Similar? _____   Scale factor: _____

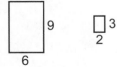

4. Similar? _____   Scale factor: _____

Name: _____   Date: _____

Unit 4: Ratio, Proportion, and Percents

Lesson 30: Fractions and Percents

Here's the Info...

A **_percent_** is a ratio that compares a number to 100. Percent means *per hundred* and is represented by the symbol %.

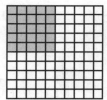

25 of 100 squares are shaded.
The shaded part of the grid represents 25%.

75 of 100 squares are white.
The white part of the grid represents 75%.

Convert fractions to percents:

Step 1: If the **_denominator_** is not 100, write a **_proportion_**. $\frac{11}{20} = \frac{x}{100}$

Step 2: Find the **_cross products_**. $1{,}100 = 20x$

Step 3: Divide both sides by 20. $\frac{1{,}100}{20} = \frac{20x}{20}$ $55 = x$

Step 4: Write a percent. $\frac{11}{20} = \frac{55}{100} = 55\%$

Convert percents to fractions:

Step 1: Write the percent as a fraction of 100. $80\% = \frac{80}{100}$

Step 2: Reduce the fraction. $\frac{80}{100} \div \frac{20}{20} = \frac{4}{5}$

Show what you know!

Write each fraction as a percent.

1. $\frac{23}{100} =$ _____

2. $\frac{29}{50} =$ _____

3. $\frac{3}{10} =$ _____

4. $\frac{7}{25} =$ _____

Write each percent as a fraction.

5. 25% = _____

6. 60% = _____

7. 5% = _____

8. 45% = _____

Name: _____ Date: _____

Unit 4: Ratio, Proportion, and Percents

Lesson 31: Decimals and Percents

Here's the Info...

The _ratio_ 25 to 100 can be expressed in many different ways.

Fraction: $\frac{25}{100}$ or $\frac{1}{4}$ **Decimal:** 0.25   **Percent:** 25%

Convert decimals to percents:

Step 1: Write the decimal as a fraction. $0.62 = \frac{62}{100}$

Step 2: Write as a percent. $0.62 = 62\%$ ◄

> **SHORT CUT!** Move the decimal point two places to the right!

Convert percents to decimals:

Step 1: Write the percent as a fraction over 100. $28\% = \frac{28}{100}$

Step 2: Write as a decimal. $28\% = 0.28$ ◄

> **SHORT CUT!** Move the decimal point two places to the left!

Show what you know!

Write each decimal as a percent.

1. 0.33 = _____   2. 0.06 = _____   3. 0.70 = _____

4. 0.68 = _____   5. 0.36 = _____   6. 0.002 = _____

7. 0.63 = _____   8. 0.375 = _____

Write each percent as a decimal.

9. 47% = _____   10. 50% = _____   11. 5% = _____

12. 100% = _____   13. 27.5% = _____   14. 1.25% = _____

15. 36% = _____   16. 1% = _____

Unit 4: Ratio, Proportion, and Percents

Lesson 32: Using and Finding Percents

Here's the Info...

Find the percent of a number.　　　　　　　　　What is 45% of 60?

Step 1:　Change the percent to a decimal.　　　45% = 0.45

Step 2:　Translate the problem into an **_equation_**.　What is 45% of 60?

$$n = 0.45 \times 60$$

Step 3:　Multiply.　　　　　　　　　　　　$n = 27$

Some problems may ask for the percent, while some may ask for the whole number. Translate each sentence carefully, then solve.

What percent of 70 is 14?

$$p \times 70 = 14$$

$$\frac{70p}{70} = \frac{14}{70}$$

$$p = 0.2 = 20\%$$

20% of 70 is 14

12 is 48% of what number?

$$12 = 0.48 \times n$$

$$\frac{12}{0.48} = \frac{0.48n}{0.48}$$

$$25 = n$$

12 is 48% of 25

Show what you know!

1. What is 80% of 75? _____
2. What is 95% of 700? _____
3. What is 20% of 54? _____
4. What is 75% of 36? _____
5. What percent of 240 is 60? _____
6. What percent of 50 is 24? _____
7. What percent of 40 is 6? _____
8. What percent of 90 is 9? _____
9. 15 is 75% of what number? _____
10. 18 is 30% of what number? _____
11. 40 is 80% of what number? _____
12. 75 is 20% of what number? _____

Name: _____ Date: _____

  # Unit 4: Ratio, Proportion, and Percents

Lesson 33: Percent Increase and Decrease

Here's the Info...

Percent of change is a measure of how a value changes in relation to the original value. If the new value is greater than the original, the change is called a *percent increase*. If the new value is less than the original, the change is called a *percent decrease*.

Find a percent increase:

Original Price: $56   New Price: $70

Step 1: Subtract to find the amount of change.   70 – 56 = 14

Step 2: Divide by the original amount.   14 ÷ 56 = 0.25

Step 3: Write as a percent.   0.25 = 25%

> Always subtract the smaller number from the larger number.

Find a percent decrease:

Original Enrollment: 72   New Enrollment: 64

Step 1: Subtract to find the amount of change.   72 – 64 = 8

Step 2: Divide by the original amount.   8 ÷ 72 = 0.11

Step 3: Write as a percent.   0.11 = 11%

Show what you know!

Find each percent increase. Round to the nearest percent.

1. 50 to 66 _____   2. 80 to 95 _____   3. 45 to 83 _____

4. 32 to 56 _____   5. 45 to 89 _____   6. 106 to 108 _____

Find each percent decrease. Round to the nearest percent.

7. 90 to 75 _____   8. 180 to 84 _____   9. 120 to 84 _____

10. 225 to 189 _____   11. 72 to 64 _____   12. 46 to 23 _____

Name: _____ Date: _____

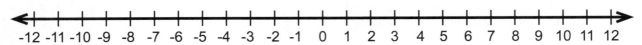

Unit 5: Integers

Lesson 34: Adding Integers

Here's the Info...

You can use a number line to help you add **_integers_**. Here's how you do it!

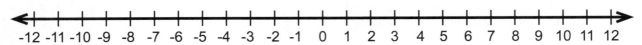

-12 -11 -10 -9 -8 -7 -6 -5 -4 -3 -2 -1 0 1 2 3 4 5 6 7 8 9 10 11 12

Find the **_sum_** of 4 and -7.

Step 1: Put your pencil on the first number in the addition problem. In this case, put your pencil on 4.

Step 2: Because you are adding a **_negative number_**, you will be moving your pencil in the negative direction or to the left. Move your pencil 7 units to the left. (Note: If you were adding a **_positive number_**, you would move in the positive direction or to the right.)

Step 3: The point that you land on after moving 7 to the left is your answer. So, the sum of 4 and -7 is -3.

Sometimes, you want to add integers that are a little bigger and you can't draw a number line that big on your paper. Here are some shortcuts to keep in mind.

Shortcut 1: If both of the integers are positive, add like usual. Your answer will be positive.
Example: 25 + 14 = 39

Shortcut 2: If both of the integers are negative, add like usual. Your answer will be negative.
Example: -15 + -31 = -46

Shortcut 3: If the integers have different signs, that is, one is positive and one is negative, find the **_difference_** of the numbers and keep the sign of the number with the greater **_absolute value_**.
Examples: -21 + 49 = 28   and   13 + (-38) = -25

Show what you know!

Find the sum.

1. 9 + (-5) = _____   2. -12 + (-26) = _____

3. -8 + 2 = _____   4. 13 + (-7) = _____

5. -32 + 56 = _____   6. -3 + (-9) = _____

7. 27 + (-29) = _____   8. -41 + 30 = _____

Name: _____ Date: _____

Unit 5: Integers

Lesson 35: Subtracting Integers

Here's the Info...

Do you like addition better than subtraction? Then subtracting **_integers_** is for you! Anytime you see an integer subtraction problem, you can rewrite it as an addition problem and use one of the two basic rules for subtracting integers.

Rule #1: Subtracting a **_negative number_** is the same as adding a **_positive number_**.

	Example 1	**Example 2**
Subtraction problem	8 – (-2)	-6 – (-4)
Rewrite as addition problem using Rule #1.	8 – (-2) = 8 + 2	-6 – (-4) = -6 + 4
Find the answer.	8 – (-2) = 8 + 2 = 10	-6 – (-4) = -6 + 4 = -2

Rule #2: Subtracting a **_positive number_** is the same as adding a **_negative number_**.

	Example 3	**Example 4**
Subtraction problem	10 – 13	-7 – 9
Rewrite as addition problem using Rule #2.	10 – 13 = 10 + (-13)	-7 – 9 = -7 + (-9)
Find the answer.	10 – 13 = 10 + (-13) = -3	-7 – 9 = -7 + (-9) = -16

Show what you know!

Find the difference.

1. 18 – (-4) = _____

2. -10 – (-28) = _____

3. -35 – (-12) = _____

4. 48 – 16 = _____

5. 27 – 39 = _____

6. -6 – 15 = _____

7. -64 – 22 = _____

8. 9 – (-16) = _____

Name: _____ Date: _____

Unit 5: Integers

Lesson 36: Multiplying and Dividing Integers

Here's the Info...

Multiplying and dividing integers is pretty much the same as multiplying and dividing whole numbers. The only difference is you have to be able to determine the sign of your answer. Here's what you need to know.

Rule #1: If the signs of the integers are the same, then the answer is positive.

Example 1	**Example 2**	**Example 3**	**Example 4**
$3 \times 5 = 15$	$-2 \times -9 = 18$	$20 \div 4 = 5$	$-32 \div -8 = 4$

Rule #2: If the signs of the integers are different, then the answer is negative.

Example 5	**Example 6**	**Example 7**	**Example 8**
$-6 \times 4 = -24$	$3 \times -7 = -21$	$30 \div -5 = -6$	$-14 \div 7 = -2$

Show what you know!

Determine whether the answer will be positive or negative. Write positive or negative in the blank.

1. $-624 \div 48$ _____

2. -462×-251 _____

3. 894×579 _____

4. $831 \div -18$ _____

5. $-520 \div -84$ _____

6. 96×-87 _____

Find the product or quotient as indicated.

7. $84 \div -12 =$ _____

8. $-6 \times 8 =$ _____

9. $-72 \div -6 =$ _____

10. $15 \times -3 =$ _____

11. $-13 \times -5 =$ _____

12. $-54 \div 9 =$ _____

Name: _____   Date: _____

Unit 5: Integers

Lesson 37: Coordinate Graphs

Here's the Info...

You can use **_integers_** to help locate points on a **_coordinate graph_**. The points are identified by an **_ordered pair_** (x, y). The first number, or the **_x-coordinate_**, tells the horizontal location of the point. The second number, or the **_y-coordinate_**, tells the vertical location of the point. A positive x-coordinate indicates a horizontal location to the right of the **_origin_**, and a negative x-coordinate indicates a horizontal location to the left. A positive y-coordinate indicates a vertical location above the origin, and a negative y-coordinate indicates a vertical location below the origin. That's a lot of information! So, let's look at some examples.

Point A is located at (3, 2). To get there from the origin, you would move 3 gridlines to the right and then up 2 gridlines.

Point B is located at (-5, -8). To get there from the origin, you would move 5 gridlines to the left and then down 8 gridlines.

What is the ordered pair that gives the location for point C?

To get to point C from the origin, you must move 6 gridlines to the right and then down 4 gridlines. So, the ordered pair that gives the location for point C is (6, -4).

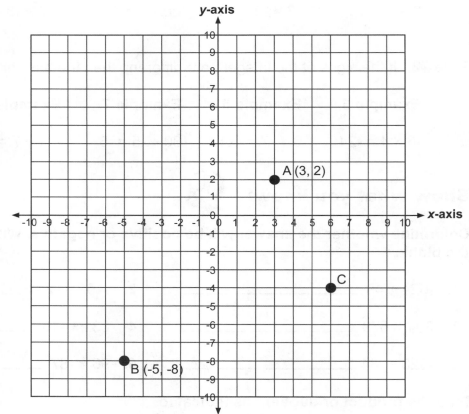

Name: _____ Date: _____

Unit 5: Integers

Lesson 37: Coordinate Graphs (cont.)

Show what you know!

Write the ordered pairs that represent the location of the following points on the coordinate grid below.

1. A _____   2. B _____   3. C _____

4. D _____   5. E _____   6. F _____

Plot the points with the given coordinates on the coordinate grid below.

7. G (4, 6)   8. H (-7, 2)   9. J (0, 9)

10. K (5, -1)   11. L (-3, -6)   12. M (-4, 0)

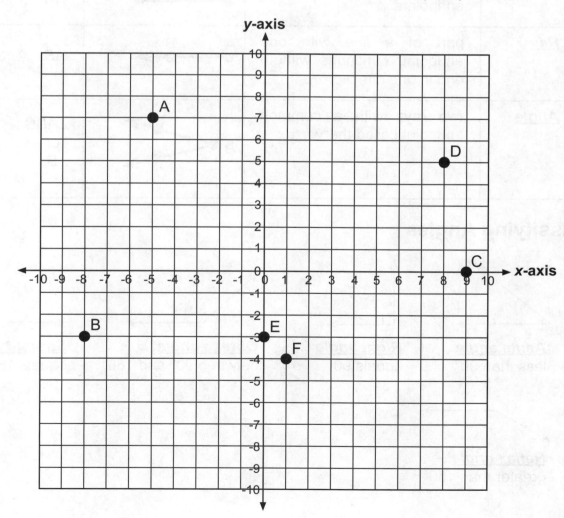

Unit 6: Geometry and Measurement Reference Pages

Basic Geometry Figures

Figure	Properties	Example	Symbol
Point	represents a position in space	● A	A
Line	continues without end in opposite directions	A B	$\overleftrightarrow{AB}$
Plane	flat surface with no thickness that continues without end in all directions	A B M D C	plane ABCD or plane M
Segment	part of a line with two endpoints	A B	$\overline{AB}$
Ray	part of a line with one endpoint; continues without end in one direction	A B	$\overrightarrow{AB}$
Angle	two rays with a common endpoint called the **_vertex_**	A B C	∠ABC or ∠B

Classifying Angles

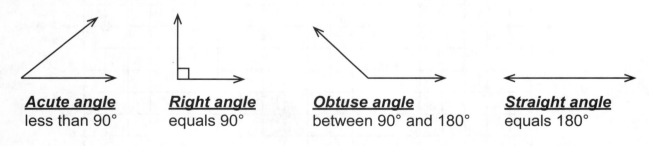

Acute angle
less than 90°

Right angle
equals 90°

Obtuse angle
between 90° and 180°

Straight angle
equals 180°

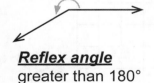

Reflex angle
greater than 180°

Unit 6: Geometry and Measurement Reference Pages

Classifying Triangles

By Angles

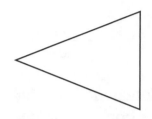

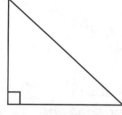

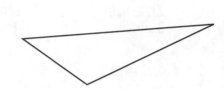

Acute triangle	*Right triangle*	*Obtuse triangle*
three acute angles	one right angle	one obtuse angle

By Sides

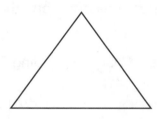

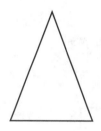

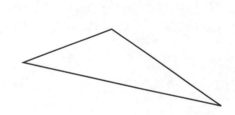

Equilateral triangle	*Isosceles triangle*	*Scalene triangle*
all sides equal	at least two sides equal	no sides equal

Polygons

A ***polygon*** is a closed figure that has three or more sides. Each side is a ***line segment*** and the sides meet only at the endpoints, or ***vertices***.

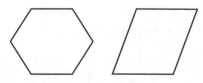

Polygons

Not Polygons

Name: _____ Date: _____

 ## Unit 6: Geometry and Measurement Reference Pages

Types of Polygons

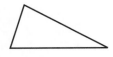

Triangle	_Quadrilateral_	_Pentagon_	_Hexagon_
3 sides	4 sides	5 sides	6 sides

Heptagon:	7 sides	_Octagon:_	8 sides	_Nonagon:_	9 sides
Decagon:	10 sides	_Dodecagon:_	12 sides	_n – gon:_	n sides

Congruent Figures

Congruent figures have the same size and shape. When two figures are congruent, their corresponding parts are congruent as well.

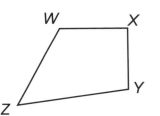

$ABCD \cong WXYZ$

Corresponding Angles

$\angle A \cong \angle W$
$\angle B \cong \angle X$
$\angle C \cong \angle Y$
$\angle D \cong \angle Z$

Corresponding Sides

$\overline{AB} \cong \overline{WX}$
$\overline{BC} \cong \overline{XY}$
$\overline{CD} \cong \overline{YZ}$
$\overline{AD} \cong \overline{WZ}$

Symmetry

A _symmetric figure_ can be folded in half so that the two halves match. Some figures have more than one line of symmetry.

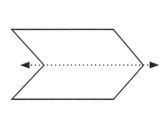

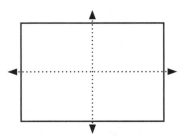

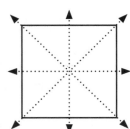

Name: _____ Date: _____

Unit 6: Geometry and Measurement Reference Pages

Transformations

A **_transformation_** is the movement of a figure in a plane.

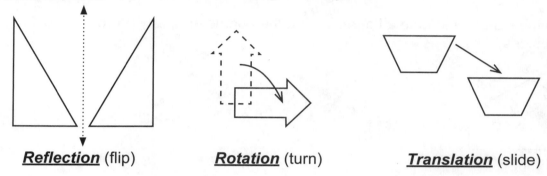

Reflection (flip)   **_Rotation_** (turn)   **_Translation_** (slide)

Standard and Metric Measure (Length, Weight, and Volume)

Type of Measure	Metric	Standard
Length	meter	inch, foot, yard, mile
Weight	gram	ounce, pound, ton
Volume	liter	cup, quart, gallon

The **_metric system_** of measurement is based on powers of ten. The prefixes are used with all types of measures.

Prefix	Meaning	Example
milli-	one thousandth	1 milliliter is 0.001 liter.
centi-	one hundredth	1 centimeter is 0.01 meter.
kilo-	one thousand	1 kilogram is 1,000 grams.

The **_standard system_** of measurement is not based on powers of ten. There are no prefixes, so some basic conversions must be memorized.

Length	Weight	Volume
12 inches = 1 foot	16 ounces = 1 pound	2 cups = 1 pint
3 feet = 1 yard	2,000 pounds = 1 ton	2 pints = 1 quart
1,760 yards = 1 mile		4 quarts = 1 gallon

Name: _____   Date: _____

Unit 6: Geometry and Measurement

Lesson 38: Perimeter

Here's the Info...

Perimeter is the distance around a figure. To find the perimeter of any polygon, add the lengths of all sides.

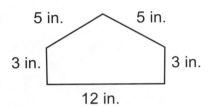

$P = 3 + 5 + 5 + 3 + 12 =$ 28 in.

Opposite sides of a **rectangle** are equal in length. Only the length and width are needed to find the perimeter.

Step 1: Use the formula $P = 2l + 2w$.

$P = 2(15) + 2(8)$

Step 2: Multiply.

$P = 30 + 16$

Step 3: Add.

$P = 46$ cm

A **square** has four sides of equal length. Only the length of one side is needed to find the perimeter.

Step 1: Use the formula $P = 4s$.

$P = 4(12)$

Step 2: Multiply.

$P = 48$ ft.

Show what you know!
Find the perimeter.

1.

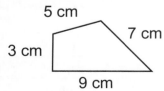

2.

3.
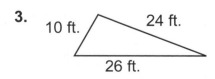

$P =$ _____ $P =$ _____ $P =$ _____

Name: _____ Date: _____

Unit 6: Geometry and Measurement

Lesson 39: Circumference

Here's the Info...

Circumference is the distance around a circle. A number close to 3.14 is used to calculate circumference. The symbol π, which is read aloud as **_pi_**, is used to represent this special number.

Some important parts of a circle are shown in the figure below:

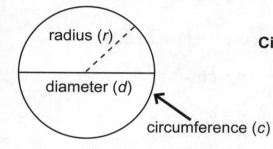

Circumference of a Circle: $C = 2\pi r$ or $C = \pi d$

To find the circumference of a circle:

Step 1: Choose a formula for circumference.

$C = 2\pi r$

Step 2: Substitute the length of the radius and 3.14 for π.

$C = 2 (3.14) (3)$

Step 3: Multiply.

$C = 18.84$ in.

Show what you know!

Find each circumference. Use 3.14 for π.

1. 14 m

2. 9 ft.

3. 8 in.

4. 2.5 cm

$C =$ _____

$C =$ _____

$C =$ _____

$C =$ _____

5. $r = 7$ in.

6. $d = 13$ cm

7. $d = 27$ m

8. $r = 3.75$ ft.

$C =$ _____

$C =$ _____

$C =$ _____

$C =$ _____

Name: _____ Date: _____

Unit 6: Geometry and Measurement

Lesson 40: Area of Rectangles and Parallelograms

Here's the Info...

Counting squares is one way to find the **_area_** of a **_rectangle_**.

Each square has an area of one square centimeter (cm^2). ➡

The area of this rectangle is 8 cm^2.

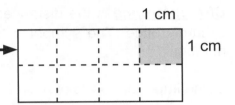

If there are too many squares to count (or no squares at all), use the formula below:

Area = base x height ➡ **A = bh**

$A = bh$
$A = (15)(2)$
$A = 30$ cm^2

To find the area of a **parallelogram**, use the same formula! Just look carefully for the height.

Possible Pitfall...

The height of a parallelogram is always **perpendicular** to the base.

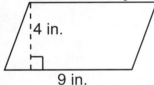   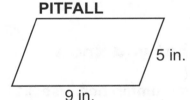

The RIGHT Way

4 in.

9 in.

$A = bh = (9)(4) =$ 36 in.^{2}

PITFALL

5 in.

9 in.

$A = bh = (9)(5) =$ 45 in.^{2}

Show what you know!

Find the area of each figure.

1. 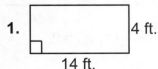   4 ft.
14 ft.

2. 5 cm 3 cm
10 cm

3. 7 in.
8 in.

4. 15 m
17 m
3.5 m

A = _____   A = _____   A = _____   A = _____

Name: _____

Date: _____

Unit 6: Geometry and Measurement

Lesson 41: Area of Triangles

Here's the Info...

A *triangle* has half the area of a *parallelogram* with the same base, *b*, and height, *h*.

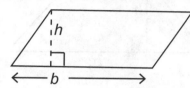 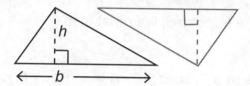

Area = base x height or **A = bh**

Area = $\frac{1}{2}$ x base x height or **A = $\frac{1}{2}$ bh**

Find the area of triangle ABC.

$A = \frac{1}{2} bh$

$A = \frac{1}{2} (10)(4) = 20$ m²

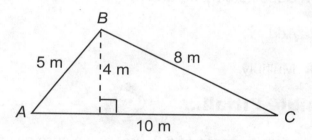

Possible Pitfall...

Be careful not to confuse the height of the triangle with one of the sides. Only in a **right triangle** can the height be the same as a side.

The RIGHT Way

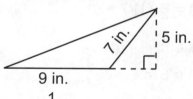

$A = \frac{1}{2} (9)(5) = 22.5$ in.²

PITFALL

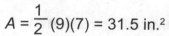

$A = \frac{1}{2} (9)(7) = 31.5$ in.²

Show what you know!

Find the area.

1.

A = _____

2.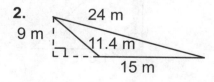

A = _____

3.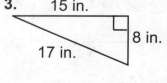

A = _____

Name: _____ Date: _____

Unit 6: Geometry and Measurement

Lesson 42: Area of Trapezoids

Here's the Info...

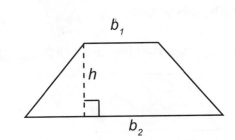

A **_trapezoid_** has two bases, labeled b_1 and b_2.

To find the area of a trapezoid, we must also know the height, h.

Area of a Trapezoid: $A = \frac{1}{2} h(b_1 + b_2)$

If $b_1 = 12$ cm, $b_2 = 16$ cm and $h = 4$ cm, find the area of the trapezoid.

Step 1: Substitute b_1, b_2, and h.

$A = \frac{1}{2} (4)(12 + 16)$

Step 2: Add.

$A = \frac{1}{2} (4)(28)$

Step 3: Multiply.

$A = 56$ cm²

Possible Pitfall...

When finding the area of a figure, make sure all of the units are the same.

Find the area of a trapezoid with $b_1 = 7$ in., $b_2 = 9$ in., and $h = 1$ ft.

The RIGHT Way

$A = \frac{1}{2} (12)(7 + 9)$

$A = \frac{1}{2} (12)(16)$

$A = 96$ in.²

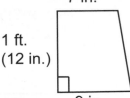

7 in.

1 ft.
(12 in.)

9 in.

PITFALL

$A = \frac{1}{2} (1)(7 + 9)$

$A = \frac{1}{2} (1)(16)$

$A = 8$ in.²

Show what you know!

Find the area of each trapezoid.

1.
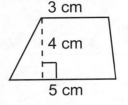
3 cm
4 cm
5 cm

$A =$ _____

2.
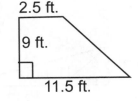
2.5 ft.
9 ft.
11.5 ft.

$A =$ _____

3.
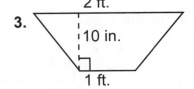
2 ft.
10 in.
1 ft.

$A =$ _____

Name: _____ Date: _____

Unit 6: Geometry and Measurement

Lesson 43: Area of Circles

Here's the Info...

To find the **area** of a circle, use the length of the **radius** (r), and the special number **pi** (π).

$r = 6$ in.

Area of a Circle: $A = \pi r^2$

Step 1: Substitute the radius length for r.

$A = \pi(6)^2$

Step 2: Square the radius.

$A = \pi(36)$

Step 3: Substitute 3.14 for π.

$A = (3.14)(36)$

Step 4: Multiply.

$A = 113.04$ in.^{2}

Possible Pitfall...

Be sure to use the radius of the circle, *not* the **diameter**. If you are given the diameter instead of the radius, remember to divide by two.

The RIGHT Way

$A = \pi r^2$
$A = \pi(4)^2$
$A = 16\pi$
$A \approx 50.24$ in.^{2}

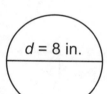

$d = 8$ in.

PITFALL

$A = \pi r^2$
$A = \pi(8)^2$
$A = 64\pi$
$A \approx 200.96$ in.^{2}

Show what you know!

Find the area of each circle. Use 3.14 for π.

1.   3 ft.

2.   10 m

3.   60 cm

4.   2 in.

$A =$ _____ $A =$ _____ $A =$ _____ $A =$ _____

Name: _____ Date: _____

Unit 6: Geometry and Measurement

Lesson 44: Surface Area of Rectangular and Triangular Prisms

Here's the Info...

The **surface area** of a solid figure is the total area of its exterior surfaces, called **faces**. Think of it as the parts of the figure that you would paint.

Use **A = bh** to find the areas of the faces. To find the surface area of a prism, find the **sum** of the areas of the faces.

Let's find the surface area of a rectangular prism. A **rectangular prism** has 6 faces. All faces are quadrilaterals. Opposite faces are equal.

Step 1: Find the area for the front face.
$A = 12 \times 4$
$A = 48$

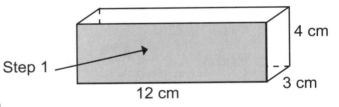

Step 2: Multiply the area of the front face by 2 (one for the front, one for the equal rear face).
$A = 2 \times 48$
$A = 96$

Step 3: Find the area for the top face. Multiply that number by 2 (one for the top face, one for the bottom face).
$A = 2(12 \times 3)$
$A = 72$

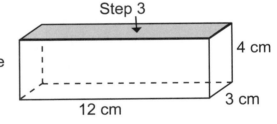

Step 4: Find the area for the right face. Multiply that number by 2 (one for the right face, one for the left face).
$A = 2(3 \times 4)$
$A = 24$

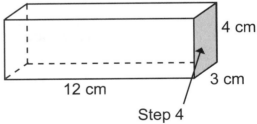

Step 5: Add the three areas together to find the surface area of the prism.
$SA = 96 + 72 + 24$
$SA = 192 \text{ cm}^2$

Name: _____ Date: _____

Unit 6: Geometry and Measurement

Lesson 44: Surface Area of Rectangular and Triangular Prisms (cont.)

So think of finding the surface area of a prism as:
SA = (number of equal faces [*bh*]) + (number of equal faces [*bh*]) + (number of equal faces [*bh*])

Now let's use that formula to find the surface area of a triangular prism. Because this prism is triangular, we use $A = \frac{1}{2} bh$ to find the area of the triangular faces.

A *triangular prism* has 5 faces. 3 faces are rectangles, and 2 faces are triangles.

SA = (number of equal faces x $\frac{1}{2}$[*bh*]) + (number of equal faces x [*bh*])

SA = [2 x ($\frac{1}{2}$ x 7 x 6)] + [3 x (10 x 7)]

SA = (2 x 21) + (3 x 70)

SA = 42 + 210

SA = 252 in.²

Show what you know!

Find the surface area of each prism.

1.
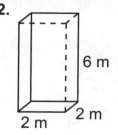
5 ft.
6 ft. 3 ft.

2.
6 m
2 m
2 m

3.
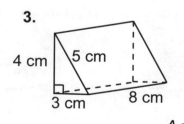
4 cm 5 cm
3 cm 8 cm

4.
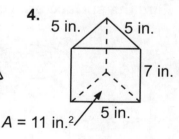
5 in. 5 in.
7 in.
5 in.
A = 11 in.²

A = _____   A = _____   A = _____   A = _____

Name: _____ Date: _____

Unit 6: Geometry and Measurement

Lesson 45: Surface Area of Cylinders

Here's the Info...

The **_surface area_** of a **_cylinder_** is the sum of the areas of a rectangle and two circles. The circular bases of the cylinder are equal in area. The height of the rectangle is the height of the cylinder. The base of the rectangle is the **_circumference_** of the cylinder.

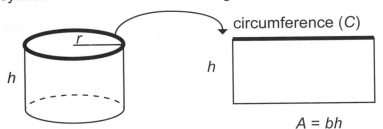

circumference (C)

$A = bh$

$A = 2(\pi r^2)$

If the radius of the cylinder above is 2 cm and the height is 5 cm, find the surface area (SA).

Step 1: Find the circumference of one circle.

$C = 2\pi r$
$C = 2(3.14)(2) = 12.56$ cm

Step 2: Find the area of the rectangle.
(Remember the base is C.)

$A = bh$
$A = (12.56)(5) = 62.8$ cm²

Step 3: Find the area of the <u>two</u> circles.

$A = 2 \times (\pi r^2)$
$A = 2 \times (3.14 \times 2^2) = 25.12$ cm²

Step 4: Add the areas.

$SA = 62.8 + 25.12 = 87.92$ cm²

Show what you know!

Find the surface area of each cylinder. Use 3.14 for π.

1.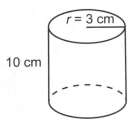

$r = 3$ cm

10 cm

$A =$ _____

2.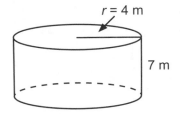

$r = 4$ m

7 m

$A =$ _____

3.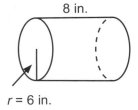

8 in.

$r = 6$ in.

$A =$ _____

Name: _____

Date: _____

Unit 6: Geometry and Measurement

Lesson 46: Volume

Here's the Info...

Volume tells us how much a container can hold in **cubic units**. To find the volume of a **prism** or **cylinder**, you can use the formula $V = Bh$, where B stands for the area of the base and h stands for the height of the prism.

Find the volume of the rectangular prism shown.

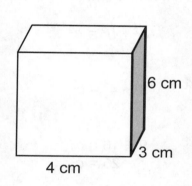

6 cm

3 cm

4 cm

Step 1: Write the volume formula.

$V = Bh$

Step 2: Rewrite it using the appropriate formula for the area of the base. Because the base is a rectangle, we can use $l \times w$ for the area of the base.

$V = l \times w \times h$

Step 3: Substitute the values for l, w, and h.

$V = 4 \times 3 \times 6$

Step 4: Multiply. Because we are finding volume, the units should be cubed. So, the volume of the rectangular prism is 72 cm³.

$V = 72 \text{ cm}^3$

To find the volume of a cylinder, use the same steps. Because the base of a cylinder is a circle, use πr^2 to find the area of the base. Here's an example.

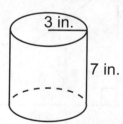

3 in.

7 in.

$V = Bh$
$V = \pi r^2 h$
$V = \pi(3^2)(7)$
$V = \pi(9)(7)$
$V = 63\pi \text{ in.}^3$
$V = 197.82 \text{ in.}^3$

Show what you know!

BEST OF SHOW

Find the volume.

1.

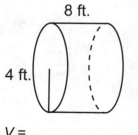

8 ft.

4 ft.

$V =$ _____

2.

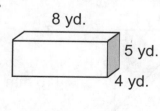

8 yd.

5 yd.

4 yd.

$V =$ _____

3.

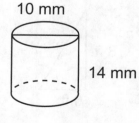

10 mm

14 mm

$V =$ _____

Name: _____ Date: _____

Unit 6: Geometry and Measurement

Lesson 47: Pythagorean Theorem

Here's the Info...

The **_Pythagorean Theorem_** shows a special relationship between the
three sides of a **_right triangle_**. It says that the **_sum_** of the **_squares_** of the
two legs of a right triangle is equal to the square of the **_hypotenuse_**. The
relationship is represented by the equation $a^2 + b^2 = c^2$. Look familiar?

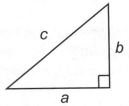

Find the length of the hypotenuse of a triangle whose legs measure 3 cm and 4 cm.

Step 1: Write the Pythagorean Theorem.

$$a^2 + b^2 = c^2$$

Step 2: Substitute the values for the lengths of the legs. The legs
are always represented by a and b, and the hypotenuse is
always represented by c.

$$3^2 + 4^2 = c^2$$

Step 3: Simplify the equation.

$$9 + 16 = c^2$$
$$25 = c^2$$

Step 4: Take the square root of each side. The length of the
hypotenuse is 5 cm.

$$\sqrt{25} = \sqrt{c^2}$$
$$5 = c$$

Now, let's find the length of one of the legs when we are given the length of the hypotenuse
and the other leg.

$$a^2 + b^2 = c^2$$
$$5^2 + b^2 = 13^2 \longrightarrow 25 + b^2 = 169$$
$$b^2 = 169 - 25$$
$$b^2 = 144 \longrightarrow \sqrt{b^2} = \sqrt{144}$$
$$b = 12 \text{ in.}$$

[Triangle with hypotenuse 13 in., leg b, and base 5 in.]

REMEMBER: The Pythagorean Theorem can only be used with RIGHT TRIANGLES.

Show what you know!
Find the missing measurements in the right triangles below.

1.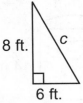
8 ft. c 6 ft.

2.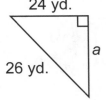
24 yd. a 26 yd.

3.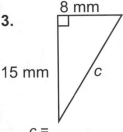
8 mm   15 mm c

4.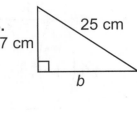
25 cm   7 cm b

$c = $ _____ $a = $ _____ $c = $ _____ $b = $ _____

Name: _____ Date: _____

Unit 6: Geometry and Measurement

Lesson 48: Angle Relationships and Intersecting Lines

Here's the Info...

When two or more lines **_intersect_**, **_angles_** are formed. Let's take a look at some of the relationships between those angles.

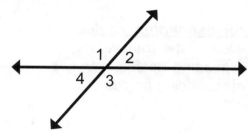

Angles 1 and 2 are known as a **_linear pair_** because they form a line.

Because they are a linear pair, they are also **_supplementary_**. Supplementary angles have a sum of 180°. Other linear pairs are ∠2 and ∠3; ∠3 and ∠4; and ∠1 and ∠4.

Angles 1 and 3 are known as **_vertical angles_** because they are opposite each other. Vertical angles have the same measure. Other vertical angles are ∠2 and ∠4.

We can use these relationships to find the measure of an angle. Let's say ∠1 has a measure of 130°, and we want to find the measure of the other three angles. We can use the properties of linear pairs and vertical angles.

$m\angle 2 = 180° - 130° = 50°$

$m\angle 3 = m\angle 1 = 130°$

$m\angle 4 = m\angle 2 = 50°$

Show what you know!

Find the measures of the angles labeled *a*, *b*, and *c* in the pictures below.

1. a = _____

b = _____

c = _____

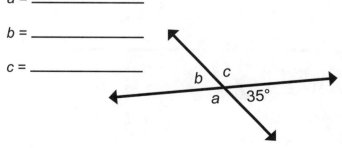

2.

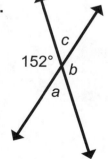

a = _____

b = _____

c = _____

Name: _____   Date: _____

Unit 6: Geometry and Measurement

Lesson 49: Angle Relationships and Parallel Lines

Here's the Info...

When **_parallel lines_** are intersected by a line known as a **_transversal_**, angles are formed that have special relationships. Let's take a look!

Angles 1 and 5 are known as **_corresponding angles_** because they are on the same side of the transversal and in the same position. Corresponding angles have the same measure. The other corresponding angles are $\angle 4$ and $\angle 8$; $\angle 2$ and $\angle 6$; and $\angle 3$ and $\angle 7$.

Angles 1 and 7 are known as **_alternate exterior angles_** because they are on opposite sides of the transversal and on the exterior of the parallel lines. Alternate exterior angles have the same measure. The other alternate exterior angles are $\angle 2$ and $\angle 8$.

Angles 4 and 6 are known as **_alternate interior angles_** because they are on the opposite sides of the transversal and on the interior of the parallel lines. Alternate interior angles have the same measure. The other alternate interior angles are $\angle 3$ and $\angle 5$.

Let's say that the measure of $\angle 1$ is 30° and the measure of $\angle 6$ is 150°. Find all of the other angle measures.

$m\angle 6 = m\angle 2 = m\angle 8 = m\angle 4 = 150°$

$m\angle 1 = m\angle 5 = m\angle 3 = m\angle 7 = 30°$

Show what you know!

Find the measures of the angles labeled *a, b, c, d, e,* and *f.*

1. $a =$ _____

2. $b =$ _____

3. $c =$ _____

4. $d =$ _____

5. $e =$ _____

6. $f =$ _____

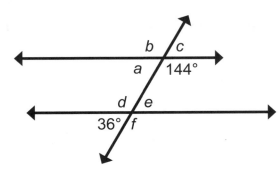

Name: _____ Date: _____

Unit 7: Probability and Statistics

Graph Reference Pages

Circle Graphs

A *circle graph* is a diagram in which data is represented as a part of a circle.

For example, this circle graph shows the percentage of people surveyed who selected each of the sports listed as their favorite sport.

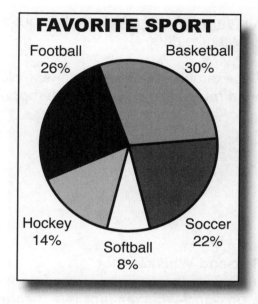

FAVORITE SPORT

Football 26%

Basketball 30%

Hockey 14%

Softball 8%

Soccer 22%

Bar Graphs

A *bar graph* is a diagram in which data is displayed using vertical or horizontal bars.

For example, these bar graphs show the number of people surveyed who selected each of the sports listed as their favorite sport.

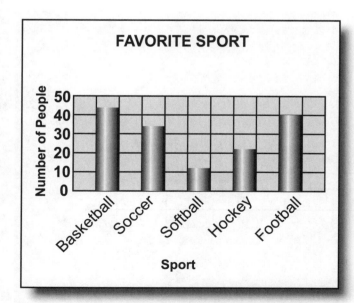

FAVORITE SPORT

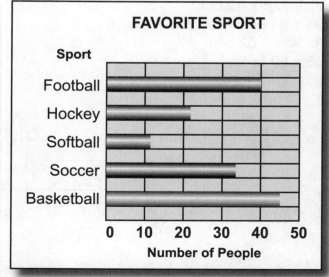

FAVORITE SPORT

Name: _____   Date: _____

Unit 7: Probability and Statistics

Graph Reference Pages (cont.)

Stem-and-Leaf Plot

A **_stem-and-leaf plot_** is a diagram that uses place value to organize data.

For example, this stem-and-leaf plot shows the resting heart rates in beats per minute (bpm) of 20 people.

4	2 3 3 8
5	4 4 6 6 9
6	2 2 5 8 8 8
7	0 0 1 1 4

Key: 4 | 2 = 42 bpm

Box-and-Whisker Plot

A **_box-and-whisker plot_** is a diagram that shows the distribution of a set of data using the minimum, maximum, quartiles, and **_median_**. The **_first quartile_** (Q1) is the median of the first half of the data and the **_third quartile_** (Q3) is the median of the second half of the data.

For example, this box-and-whisker plot shows the distribution of the heart rates in beats per minute (bpm) of 20 people.

Minimum = 42 bpm
Q1 = 54 bpm
Median = 62 bpm
Q3 = 69 bpm
Maximum = 74 bpm

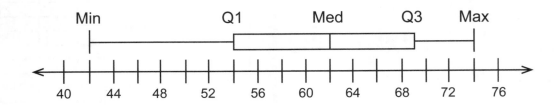

Name: _____ Date: _____

Unit 7: Probability and Statistics

Lesson 50: Measures of Central Tendency

Here's the Info...

There are three measures of central tendency, and each one is used to give different information about a set of data. Let's find the measures of central tendency for the data set:

5   8   4   6   5   9   5

The **_mean_** is the arithmetic **_average_** of a data set. Find the mean of the given data set.

Step 1:   Add all of the values together. $5 + 8 + 4 + 6 + 5 + 9 + 5 = 42$

Step 2:   Divide by the number of values in the
            data set. The mean of this data set is 6. $42 \div 7 = 6$

The **_mode_** is the number that occurs most frequently in the data set. Sometimes a data set has two numbers that occur with the same frequency. This data set is **_bimodal_**.

The data value 5 appears 3 times in the data set. No other value appears that many times. Therefore, 5 is the mode.

The **_median_** is the number that is in the middle of a data set when the numbers are listed in order from least to greatest. Find the median of the given data set.

Step 1:   Put the numbers in order from least to greatest.   4   5   5   ⑤   6   8   9

Step 2:   Find the number that is in the middle of the
            data set. The median of this data set is 5.

For a data set with an **_even_** number of data values, there are two data values in the middle. So, the median is the average of the middle numbers. Look at the data set below.

2   3   3   ④   ⑥   7   8   9

The data values 4 and 6 are in the middle of the data set. So, we take their average to find the median. The sum of 4 and 6 is 10, and 10 divided by 2 is 5. Therefore, the median is 5.

Show what you know!

Find the measures of central tendency for each of the given data sets.

1. 6, 8, 6, 6, 8, 10, 5   mean = _____   median = _____   mode = _____

2. 2, 7, 3, 6, 2   mean = _____   median = _____   mode = _____

3. 5, 7, 9, 1, 5, 5, 7, 9   mean = _____   median = _____   mode = _____

Unit 7: Probability and Statistics

Lesson 51: Possible Outcomes

Here's the Info...

Let's say your uncle owns a sandwich shop. He can make sandwiches on wheat or white bread. He offers turkey, ham, bologna, and salami for the sandwiches. He wants to know how many different types of sandwiches he can make if he uses one type of bread and one type of meat on each sandwich. He asks you to help him figure out how many **possible outcomes** there are for sandwiches.

You can use a **tree diagram** to help you organize. Start by listing the two different breads. Then, make a branch off of each bread type for the four different types of meat.

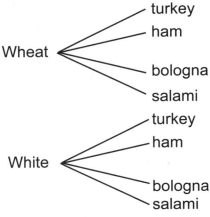

As you can see from the diagram, your uncle can make 4 different kinds of sandwiches on each of the types of bread. This makes a total of 8 possible outcomes.

You may be wondering: Isn't there a faster way?

Yes, there is! To find the number of possible sandwich choices, you can simply multiply the number of bread choices by the number of meat choices.

$$\underbrace{2}_{\text{types of bread}} \times \underbrace{4}_{\text{types of meat}} = \underbrace{8}_{\text{number of possible sandwich choices}}$$

Show what you know!

Find the number of possible outcomes. You can use a tree diagram to help you.

1. **Cones:** Sugar, Cake, Waffle
   Ice cream flavor: Chocolate, Strawberry, Vanilla
   How many different one-scoop ice cream cones can you make? _____

2. **Pants:** Blue, Black
   Shirts: Red, Green, Orange
   Hats: Purple, Yellow, Gray
   How many different outfits can you make with 1 pair of pants, 1 shirt, and 1 hat? _____

3. **Number of doors:** 2-door, 4-door
   Colors: White, Black, Red, Blue, Green, Orange
   How many different cars can you make? _____

Name: _____   Date: _____

Unit 7: Probability and Statistics

Lesson 52: Simple Probability

Here's the Info...

Probability is the chance that something will happen. It is usually expressed as a **_ratio_** of the number of favorable outcomes to the number of possible outcomes.

Let's say you're playing a game with a friend. You spin a spinner like the one shown to determine how many spaces you can move. You need a 6 to win the game. What is the probability that you will get a 6 and win the game?

Step 1: Determine the number of possible outcomes, which is also known as the **_sample space_**. There are 5 different sections on the spinner. So, the number of possible outcomes is 5.

Number of possible outcomes = 5

Step 2: Determine the number of favorable outcomes. There is only 1 section on the spinner that is labeled 6. So, there is only 1 favorable outcome.

Number of favorable outcomes = 1

Step 3: Find the probability by writing a ratio of favorable outcomes to possible outcomes. There is 1 favorable outcome and 5 possible outcomes. So, the probability that you will spin a 6 and win the game is $\frac{1}{5}$ or $P(\text{win}) = \frac{1}{5}$.

$$\frac{\text{Number of favorable outcomes}}{\text{Number of possible outcomes}} = \frac{1}{5}$$

Show what you know!
Use the spinner to answer the questions below.

1. What is the probability that the spinner lands on a 2?

   $P(2) =$ _____

2. What is the probability that the spinner lands on an odd number? $P(\text{odd}) =$ _____

3. What is the probability that the spinner lands on a number less than 5? $P(\text{less than 5}) =$ _____

Name: _____ Date: _____

Unit 7: Probability and Statistics

Lesson 53: Independent and Dependent Events

Here's the Info...

Let's say you are playing a game with a friend. On your turn, you must roll a die and spin a spinner. What is the probability that you will roll a 4 and the spinner will land on green?

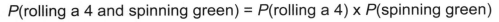

These events are known as **_independent events_**. That is, the outcome of the first event, rolling the die, does not affect the outcome of the second event, spinning the spinner.

You find the probability of each event and then multiply these probabilities to find the probability of both events.

P(rolling a 4 and spinning green) = P(rolling a 4) x P(spinning green)

$$= \frac{1}{6} \times \frac{1}{4}$$
$$= \frac{1}{24}$$

Now, let's say your teacher places 5 blue balls and 4 red balls in a bag. You draw out a blue ball on your first draw. Without replacing that ball, you draw out a second ball. What is the probability that the next ball you pull out will be red?

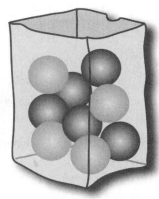

These events are known as **_dependent events_**. That is, the outcome of the first event, the color of the first ball, affects the outcome of the second event, the color of the second ball.

You find the probability of the first event and multiply that by the probability of the second event, given that the first event has already occurred.

P(blue ball and then red ball) = P(blue ball) x P(red ball given blue ball)

$$= \frac{5}{9} \times \frac{4}{8}$$
$$= \frac{20}{72}$$
$$= \frac{5}{18}$$

Name: _____ Date: _____

Unit 7: Probability and Statistics

Lesson 53: Independent and Dependent Events (cont.)

Show what you know!

Your teacher writes each letter of the word PROBABILITY on separate pieces of paper and places them in a box. Count the <u>Y</u> as a consonant for this activity. Determine whether the events below are independent or dependent. Then find the probability. Give your answer in simplest form.

| P | R | O | B | A | B | I | L | I | T | Y |

1. You draw the letter **A** on your first draw. You replace it and then draw a second letter. What is the probability that you draw **B** on your second draw?

   Are the events independent or dependent? _____

   P(draw **A** and then draw **B**) = _____

2. You draw the letter **P** on your first draw. You do not replace it and then draw a second letter. What is the probability that you draw a consonant on your second draw?

   Are the events independent or dependent? _____

   P(draw **P** and then draw a consonant) = _____

3. You draw the letter **I** on your first draw. You replace it and then draw a second letter. What is the probability that you draw a vowel on your second draw?

   Are the events independent or dependent? _____

   P(draw **I** and then draw a vowel) = _____

4. You draw the letter **B** on your first draw. You do not replace it and then draw a second letter. What is the probability that you draw an **I** on your second draw?

   Are the events independent or dependent? _____

   P(draw **B** and then draw **I**) = _____

Determine whether the events below are independent or dependent. Then find the probability. Give your answer in simplest form.

5. You flip a coin and it lands heads up. Then you roll a die. What is the probability that you roll a 2 on the die?

   Are the events independent or dependent? _____

   P(heads and then 2) = _____

6. You flip a coin and it lands heads up. You flip the coin again. What is the probability that it will land heads up on the second flip?

   Are the events independent or dependent? _____

   P(heads and then heads) = _____

Name: _____ Date: _____

Unit 8: Linear Equations

Lesson 54: Solving One-Step Equations by Adding and Subtracting

Here's the Info...

Addition and subtraction are **_inverse operations_**. You can use inverse operations to find missing values in an **_equation_**. As long as the same operation is used on both sides of an equation, the equation remains balanced.

Let's find the solution to the equation $x + 12 = 23$ by using subtraction to "undo" the addition.

Step 1:	Isolate the **_variable_** using the inverse operation. In this case, subtract 12 from each side.	$x + 12 = 23$ $\underline{-12 \quad -12}$
Step 2:	Simplify each side.	$x + 0 = 11$ $x = 11$
Step 3:	Substitute to check. Because 11 + 12 is equal to 23, we know that 11 must be the value of x.	$11 + 12 \overset{?}{=} 23$ $23 = 23$

Now, let's find the solution to the equation $y - 9 = 17$ by using addition to "undo" the subtraction.

Step 1:	Isolate the variable using the inverse operation. In this case, add 9 to each side.	$y - 9 = 17$ $\underline{+9 \quad +9}$
Step 2:	Simplify each side.	$y + 0 = 26$ $y = 26$
Step 3:	Substitute to check. Because 26 – 9 is equal to 17, we know that 26 must be the value of x.	$26 - 9 \overset{?}{=} 17$ $17 = 17$

Show what you know!

Solve each addition equation. Work the problems on your own paper.

1. $x + 23 = 48$ _____
2. $a + 14 = 25$ _____
3. $g + 13 = -54$ _____

Solve each subtraction equation. Work the problems on your own paper.

4. $b - 33 = 20$ _____
5. $p - 9 = 56$ _____
6. $n - 4 = -9$ _____

Solve each equation. Work the problems on your own paper.

7. $v - 87 = 21$ _____
8. $c + 49 = 30$ _____
9. $x + 13 = -5$ _____

 © Mark Twain Media, Inc., Publishers 70

Name: _____ Date: _____

Unit 8: Linear Equations

Lesson 55: Solving One-Step Equations by Multiplying and Dividing

Here's the Info...

Multiplication and division are **_inverse operations_**. You can use inverse operations to find missing values in an **_equation_**. As long as the same operation is used on both sides of an equation, the equation remains balanced.

Let's find the solution to the equation $9n = 108$ by using division to "undo" the multiplication.

Step 1: Isolate the **_variable_** using the inverse operation. In this case, divide each side by 9.

$$\frac{9n}{9} = \frac{108}{9}$$

Step 2: Simplify each side.

$$1n = 12$$
$$n = 12$$

Step 3: Substitute to check. Because 9 x 12 is equal to 108, we know that 12 must be the value of n.

$$9(12) \overset{?}{=} 108$$
$$108 = 108$$

Now, let's find the solution to the equation $\frac{a}{3} = 14$ by using multiplication to "undo" the division.

Step 1: Isolate the variable using the inverse operation. In this case, multiply each side by 3.

$$\cancel{3} \cdot \frac{a}{\cancel{3}} = 14 \cdot 3$$

Step 2: Simplify each side. In this case, multiplication by three cancels division by three.

$$a = 42$$

Step 3: Substitute to check. Because 42 ÷ 3 is equal to 14, we know that 42 must be the value of a.

$$\frac{42}{3} \overset{?}{=} 14$$
$$14 = 14$$

Show what you know!

Solve each multiplication equation. Work the problems on your own paper.

1. $8x = 48$

2. $4p = 64$

3. $3h = -12$

4. $-10d = 100$

_____   _____   _____   _____

Solve each division equation. Work the problems on your own paper.

5. $\frac{m}{4} = 13$

6. $\frac{b}{6} = 120$

7. $\frac{w}{12} = -2$

8. $\frac{x}{-3} = 5$

_____   _____   _____   _____

Name: _____ Date: _____

Unit 8: Linear Equations

Lesson 56: Solving Two-Step Equations

Here's the Info...

Some equations contain more than one operation. The equation $4x - 7 = 13$ contains both multiplication and subtraction. To find the missing value in the equation, we should use ***inverse operations***, but which operation should we "undo" first?

Experience tells us that it is much easier to undo addition and subtraction first. Here's how it works:

Step 1: Isolate the ***term*** that contains the ***variable*** using the inverse operation. In this case, add 7 to both sides.

$$\begin{array}{r} 4x - 7 = 13 \\ + 7 \quad + 7 \end{array}$$

Step 2: Simplify each side.

$$4x = 20$$

Step 3: Now, isolate the variable using the inverse operation. Here we will divide each side by 4.

$$\frac{4x}{4} = \frac{20}{4}$$

Step 4: Simplify each side.

$$x = 5$$

Step 5: Substitute to check, using the ***order of operations*** carefully. Because $4(5) - 7$ is equal to 13, we know that 5 is the value of x.

$$\begin{array}{r} 4(5) - 7 \stackrel{?}{=} 13 \\ 20 - 7 = 13 \\ 13 = 13 \end{array}$$

Possible Pitfall...

Every time you add, subtract, multiply, or divide a number on one side of the equation, you must do the same thing to the other side.

Subtract three from *each* side to keep the equation balanced.

The RIGHT Way

$$\begin{array}{r} 2n + 3 = 11 \\ - 3 \quad - 3 \\ \hline \frac{2n}{2} = \frac{8}{2} \\ n = 4 \end{array}$$

Subtracting the three from each side keeps the equation balanced.

PITFALL

$$\begin{array}{r} 2n + 3 = 11 \\ - 3 \\ \hline \frac{2n}{2} = \frac{11}{2} \\ n = 5.5 \end{array}$$

Show what you know!

Solve each equation. Work the problems on your own paper.

1. $5t + 10 = 25$ 2. $12p - 3 = 21$ 3. $2n + 15 = 1$ 4. $6x + 11 = 29$

_____   _____   _____   _____

5. $\frac{y}{4} - 3 = 7$ 6. $\frac{b}{5} + 8 = 23$ 7. $\frac{n}{4} + 2 = 9$ 8. $\frac{a}{2} + 11 = 9$

_____   _____   _____   _____

Name: _____ Date: _____

Unit 8: Linear Equations

Lesson 57: Graphing Linear Equations

Here's the Info...

A *linear equation* has two variables, x and y. Any point (x, y) that works in the equation is called a solution. Since there are so many solutions to a linear equation, the best way to show them all is on a graph. When you have the right points, they will form a line. That's why they are called *linear* equations!

Step 1:   To graph the equation $y = 2x + 3$, let's start by choosing some values for the variable x and then using the equation to find the corresponding values of y. It's a good idea to make a table to organize your work. It doesn't matter what values you choose for x, because all ordered pairs for a linear equation will fall on the line. It is best to choose values that are located on your graph.

Choose a value of x.	Substitute the value into the equation.	Solve for y.	Write as an *ordered pair*.
-2	$y = 2(-2) + 3$	$y = -1$	(-2, -1)
0	$y = 2(0) + 3$	$y = 3$	(0, 3)
1	$y = 2(1) + 3$	$y = 5$	(1, 5)

Step 2:   Plot the ordered pairs as points on a *coordinate plane* and draw a line to connect them. The graph of the line represents all points (x, y) that make the equation true.

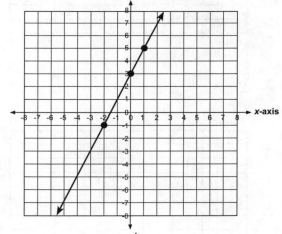

After you get the hang of it, you can make a much smaller table to show the values of x you choose and their corresponding values of y. You might even use the table feature of a graphing calculator to fill in your table.

Equation: $y = 3x - 4$

Table:

x	y
-1	-7
0	-4
2	2

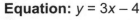

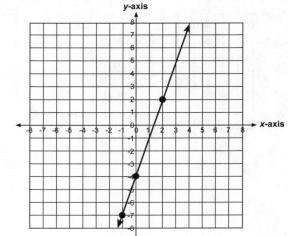

Name: _____ Date: _____

Unit 8: Linear Equations

Lesson 57: Graphing Linear Equations (cont.)

Show what you know!

Graph each linear equation.

1. $y = 3x - 1$

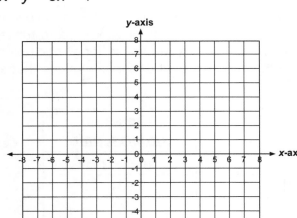

2. $y = -2x + 3$

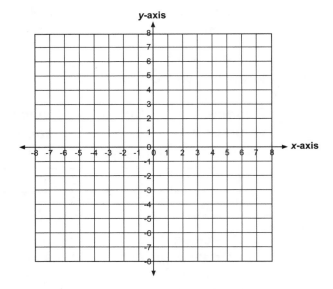

3. $y = x - 5$

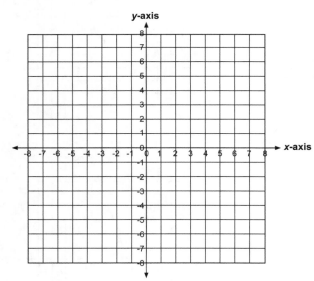

4. $y = \frac{1}{2}x + 3$

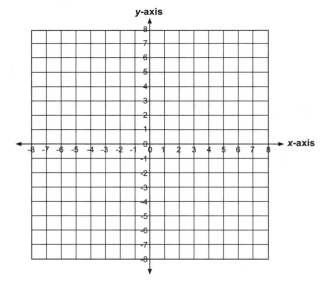

Name: _____ Date: _____

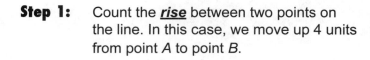

Lesson 58: Slope

Here's the Info...

Slope is a measure of the steepness of a line. To describe the slope of a line, look at how the line changes from one point to another when you move from left to right. Let's look at two different ways to do that.

Let's start by looking at the **graph** of a line.

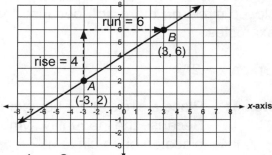

Step 1: Count the *rise* between two points on the line. In this case, we move up 4 units from point *A* to point *B*.

Step 2: Count the *run* between the same two points. In this case, we move right 6 units from *A* to *B*.

Step 3: Slope is the ratio of rise to run. $\text{slope} = \dfrac{\text{rise}}{\text{run}} = \dfrac{4}{6} = \dfrac{2}{3}$

Now, let's find the slope using **two points** on the line, *A* (-3, 2) and *B* (3, 6).

Step 1: Calculate the rise by subtracting the *y*-coordinates of the two points. $6 - 2 = 4$

Step 2: Calculate the run by subtracting the *x*-coordinates of the two points. $3 - (-3) = 6$

Step 3: Slope is the ratio of these two differences. $\text{Slope} = \dfrac{\textit{difference in y-coordinates}}{\textit{difference in x-coordinates}} = \dfrac{4}{6} = \dfrac{2}{3}$

Notice that if you subtract the coordinates starting with point *A*, the result is the same.

$$\text{Slope} = \frac{2 - 6}{-3 - (-3)} = \frac{-4}{-6} = \frac{2}{3}$$

Shortcut: A horizontal line, such as one that has the points (1, 3) and (-6, 3), always has a slope of 0. A vertical line, such as one that has the points (4, 2) and (4, 4), never has a slope.

Show what you know!

Find the slope of the line that contains the given points.

1. (-1, 7) and (4, 2)

2. (-3, -4) and (1, 2)

3. (-2, 0) and (4, -3)

_____

_____

_____

4. (-5, 2) and (1, 4)

5. (-1, 4) and (5, 4)

6. (6, 3) and (6, -3)

_____

_____

_____

Unit 9: Linear Inequalities

Lesson 59: Graphing Inequalities on a Number Line

Here's the Info...

You can graph an **_inequality_** on a number line. There are just a couple of things to keep in mind. If the inequality symbol is > or <, then you will use an open circle on the graph because the number is not included in the graph. If the inequality symbol is ≥ or ≤, then you will use a closed circle on the graph because the number is included in the graph. Let's look at some examples.

Graph $x > 2$.

Step 1: Place a circle at the number in the equality. Because the inequality symbol is >, we will place an open circle at 2.

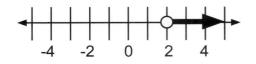

Step 2: Draw an arrow to point toward the appropriate values on the number line. Because the inequality states that x is greater than 2, we will point the arrow to the right of 2.

Let's look at another example.

Graph $z ≤ -1$.

Step 1: Place a closed circle at -1, because the inequality symbol is ≤.

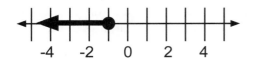

Step 2: Draw the arrow pointing to the left of -1, because z is less than or equal to -1.

Show what you know!

Graph the following inequalities.

1. $x ≥ 0$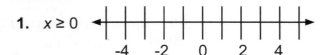

2. $y < 5$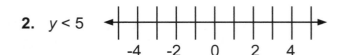

3. $r ≤ -2$

4. $s > -4$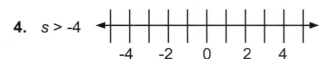

5. $t < -2$

6. $p ≥ 4$

Name: _____ Date: _____

Unit 9: Linear Inequalities

Lesson 60: Solving One-Step Inequalities by Adding and Subtracting

Here's the Info...

The steps for solving an **_inequality_** are very similar to those for solving an **equation**. **_Inverse operations_** like addition and subtraction can be used to find missing values. The biggest difference is that there will be many possible values of the variable instead of just one. A **_number line graph_** is a nice way to show them all at one time.

Let's solve the inequality $x - 5 \leq 3$ by using addition to "undo" the subtraction.

Step 1: Isolate the **_variable_** using the inverse operation. In this case, add 5 to each side.

$$\begin{array}{r} x - 5 \leq 3 \\ + 5\ + 5 \\ \hline \end{array}$$

Step 2: Simplify each side.

$$x + 0 \leq 8$$
$$x \leq 8$$

Step 3: Create a number line graph to represent the solutions. Use a <u>solid</u> circle to represent the solution that is equal to 8, then draw the arrow to point to the left to show all values less than 8.

Now, let's solve the inequality $y + 6 > 11$ by using subtraction to "undo" the addition.

Step 1: Isolate the variable using the inverse operation. In this case, subtract 6 from each side.

$$\begin{array}{r} y + 6 > 11 \\ - 6\ - 6 \\ \hline \end{array}$$

Step 2: Simplify each side.

$$y + 0 > 5$$
$$y > 5$$

Step 3: Create a number line graph. An <u>open</u> circle with the arrow pointing to the right shows that every value greater than 5 is a solution, but not 5 itself.

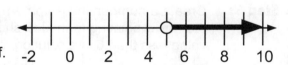

Show what you know!

Solve each inequality. Graph each solution on a number line on your own paper.

1. $x + 6 \leq 7$ 2. $b - 3 > 1$ 3. $d + 9 \geq 5$ 4. $w + 3 < -2$

_____   _____   _____   _____

5. $y - 1 \geq 4$ 6. $p + 14 \leq 20$ 7. $h - 12 > -10$ 8. $n + 23 \geq 18$

_____   _____   _____   _____

Name: _____ Date: _____

Unit 9: Linear Inequalities

Lesson 61: Solving One-Step Inequalities by Multiplying and Dividing

Here's the Info...

Inequalities that contain multiplication or division can be solved using **inverse operations**. The steps are very similar to those used to solve an **equation**. Be aware that you will have many solutions rather than just one. Use a **number line graph** to show them all at one time.

Let's solve the inequality $5x \le 20$ by using division to "undo" the multiplication.

Step 1: Isolate the **variable** using the inverse operation. In this case, divide each side by 5.

$$\frac{5x}{5} \le \frac{20}{5}$$

Step 2: Simplify each side.

$1x \le 4$

$x \le 4$

Step 3: Create a number line graph to represent the solutions. Use a <u>solid</u> circle to represent the solution that is equal to 4, then draw the arrow pointing to the left to show all values less than 4.

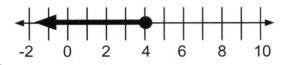

Now, let's solve the inequality $\frac{w}{-2} > -3$ by using multiplication to "undo" the division.

Step 1: Isolate the variable using the inverse operation. In this case, multiply each side by -2.

$$-2 \cdot \frac{w}{-2} > -3 \cdot -2$$

Step 2: Simplify each side. **If you multiply or divide by a negative number, reverse the inequality sign.**

$w < 6$

Step 3: Create a number line graph. An <u>open</u> circle with the arrow pointing to the left shows that every value less than 6 is a solution, but not 6 itself.

Show what you know!

Solve each inequality. Graph each solution on a number line on your own paper.

1. $9x > 36$

2. $\frac{b}{3} \le 1$

3. $-3c > -12$

4. $-20f \ge 100$

_____   _____   _____   _____

5. $\frac{m}{-3} < 2$

6. $4t \le -8$

7. $\frac{d}{2} > -2$

8. $\frac{x}{3} < 1$

_____   _____   _____   _____

Glossary

A

Absolute value: The distance that a number is from zero on a number line. It is always positive. For example, the absolute value of -5 is 5, or $|-5| = 5$, because -5 is 5 units from 0 on the number line.

Acute angle: An angle with measure less than 90°. See Unit 6 reference page 46 for an example.

Acute triangle: A triangle with three acute angles. See Unit 6 reference page 46 for an example.

Alternate exterior angles: Angles formed by the intersection of a transversal and parallel lines. They are on opposite sides of the transversal and on the exterior of the parallel lines. Alternate exterior angles have the same measure. For example, angles 1 and 7 below are alternate exterior angles.

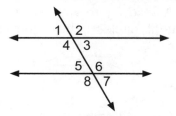

Alternate interior angles: Angles formed by the intersection of a transversal and parallel lines. They are on opposite sides of the transversal and on the interior of the parallel lines. Alternate interior angles have the same measure. For example, angles 4 and 6 above are alternate interior angles.

Angle: Two rays with a common endpoint. An angle is named using three letters or just the letter of the vertex. See Unit 6 reference page 46 for an example.

Area: A way to measure the amount of surface inside a figure. The area of the rectangle at right is 8 square units.

Average: A statistic found by taking the sum of all of the data values and then dividing it by the number of data values. For example, the average of 3, 4, and 5 is $(3 + 4 + 5) \div 3 = 4$.

B

Bar graph: A diagram in which data is displayed using vertical or horizontal bars. See Unit 7 reference page 63 for examples.

Base: A number or variable used as a repeated factor when working with exponents. For example, 2 is the base of the expression 2^3 and x is the base of the expression x^4.

Bimodal: A data set that has two modes. For example, the data set 2, 3, 3, 8, 9, 9 is bimodal. 3 and 9 are the modes.

Box-and-whisker plot: A diagram that shows the distribution of a set of data using the minimum, maximum, quartiles, and median. See Unit 7 reference page 64 for an example.

C

Circle graph: A diagram in which data is represented as a part of a circle. See Unit 7 reference page 63 for an example.

Circumference: The distance around a circle. The formula $C = 2\pi r$ or $C = \pi d$ can be used to find the circumference of a circle.

Coefficient: A number multiplied by a variable. For example, 3 is the coefficient of the expression $3x^2$.

Common denominator: A multiple of the denominators of two or more fractions. For example, 24 is a common denominator of $\frac{5}{6}$ and $\frac{3}{8}$.

Composite number: A number with more than two factors. For example, 12 is a composite number, because it has the factors 1, 2, 3, 4, 6, and 12.

Congruent figures: Two figures that have the same size and shape. See Unit 6 reference page 48 for an example.

Coordinate graph or coordinate plane: A coordinate graph is a plane with two axes, the *x*-axis and the *y*-axis, that are perpendicular to one another and intersect at a point known as the origin. The axes divide the graph into four quadrants. Points can be plotted on a coordinate plane by using coordinates in the form (*x, y*).

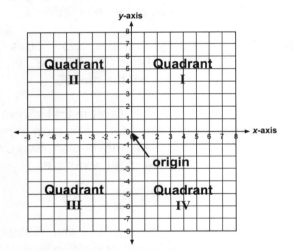

Corresponding angles: Angles formed by the intersection of a transversal and parallel lines. They are on the same side of the transversal and in the same position. Corresponding angles have the same measure. For example, angles 1 and 5 below are corresponding angles.

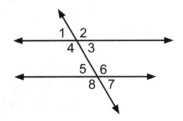

Corresponding sides: Matching sides in two congruent or similar figures. For example, the two vertical sides marked in the similar figures below are corresponding sides.

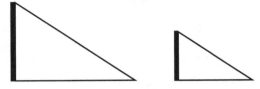

Counting numbers: The numbers used to count (1, 2, 3, 4, etc.); also called natural numbers.

Cross product: The result of multiplying the numerator of one fraction by the denominator of another fraction. For example, the proportion $\frac{2}{3} = \frac{4}{6}$ has cross products 2 x 6 and 4 x 3.

Cubic units: A unit for measuring volume. For example, cubic centimeters, or cm³, is a cubic unit.

Cylinder: A solid figure with two faces that are congruent circles. The figure below is a cylinder.

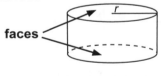

Decagon: A polygon with ten sides.

Dependent events: Events in which the outcome of the first event affects the outcome of the second event. For example, a card is drawn from a deck of cards. Without replacing the first, a second card is drawn. The probability that the second card is a heart depends on what the first card was.

Denominator: The bottom number of a fraction. For example, 5 is the denominator of the fraction $\frac{3}{5}$.

Diameter: A segment joining two points on the circle and passing through the center of the circle.

Difference: The result of a subtraction problem. For example, 6 is the difference in $8 - 2 = 6$.

Dividend: The number to be divided in a division problem. For example, 8 is the dividend in the division problem $8 \div 2 = 4$.

Divisor: The number by which the dividend is divided in a division problem. For example, 2 is the divisor in the division problem $8 \div 2 = 4$.

Dodecagon: A polygon with twelve sides.

Equation: A mathematical sentence containing an equal sign. For example, $2x + 4 = 10$ is an equation.

Equilateral triangle: A triangle with all sides equal in length. See Unit 6 reference page 47 for an example.

Equivalent fractions: Different fractions that name the same amount. For example, $\frac{4}{10}$ and $\frac{6}{15}$ are equivalent fractions, because they both represent $\frac{2}{5}$ of a whole.

Evaluate: To calculate the value.

Even: A number that is divisible by 2. For example, 2, 8, 16, and 50 are even numbers.

Exponent: A number used to show repeated multiplication of a number called the base. For example, 5 is the exponent of the expression 3^5, and it means to multiply 3 by itself 5 times, or $3 \times 3 \times 3 \times 3 \times 3$.

Expression: A mathematical statement that may use numbers, variables, or both. For example, $2y^3$ and $x^2 + 3z$ are expressions.

Faces: The exterior surfaces of a solid figure.

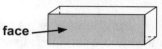

Factor: A number that divides evenly into a larger number. For example, 2 is a factor of 10 because $10 \div 2 = 5$.

First quartile (Q1): The median of the first half of a data set. For example, 3 is the first quartile of the data set, 2, 3, 5, 8, 9, 12, 13.

Greatest common factor (GCF): The largest number that is a factor of two or more numbers. For example, 8 is the GCF of 16 and 24.

Heptagon: A polygon with seven sides.

Hexagon: A polygon with six sides. See Unit 6 reference page 48 for an example.

Hypotenuse: The longest side of a right triangle. It is opposite the right angle.

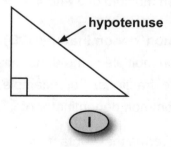

Improper fraction: A fraction in which the numerator is greater than the denominator. For example, $\frac{12}{5}$ is an improper fraction.

Independent events: Events in which the outcome of the first event does not affect the outcome of the second event. For example, a six-sided number cube is rolled and a coin is flipped. The outcome of the coin flipping is independent of the number rolled on the number cube.

Inequality: A mathematical expression that shows that two quantities are not equal. For example, $x \le 2$ and $16 > -1$ are inequalities.

Integers: Positive and negative whole numbers and 0, but no fractions or decimals. For example, -10, 0, and 342 are integers.

Intersect: To cross over one another or overlap. For example, the lines below intersect each other.

Inverse operations: Operations that "undo" each other. For example, addition and subtraction are inverse operations.

Isosceles triangle: A triangle with at least two sides equal in length. See Unit 6 reference page 47 for an example.

Least common multiple (LCM): The smallest multiple that two or more numbers have in common. For example, 12 is the least common multiple of 3 and 4.

Least common denominator (LCD): The least common multiple of the denominators of two or more fractions. For example, 18 is the least common denominator of $\frac{5}{6}$ and $\frac{2}{9}$.

Like terms: Terms that contain the same variable with the same exponent. For example, $3x^2$ and $15x^2$ are like terms.

Line: Continues without end in opposite directions. Two points are used to name a line. See Unit 6 reference page 46 for an example.

Linear equation: An equation for which the graph is a line. A linear equation has two variables, x and y. For example, the equation $y = 2x + 7$ is a linear equation.

Linear pair: Two angles that form a line. The sum of the measure of the angles in a linear pair is 180°. For example, angles 1 and 2 below are a linear pair.

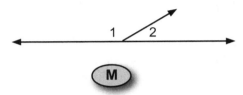

Mean: The arithmetic average of a data set. For example, the mean of the data set 6, 8, 12, and 18 is $\frac{6 + 8 + 12 + 18}{4} = 11$.

Median: The number that is in the middle of a data set when the numbers are listed in order from least to greatest. For example, 5 is the mean of the data set 1, 2, 5, 8, 13.

Metric System: A system of measurement based on powers of ten. Meters, grams, and liters are examples of metric units of measurement. See Unit 6 reference page 49 for more examples.

Mode: The number that occurs most frequently in the data set. For example, 9 is the mode of the data set 4, 5, 9, 9, 9, 12.

Multiples: Numbers found by multiplying a number by counting numbers. For example, 5, 10, 15, 20, etc. are multiples of 5.

Negative number: A number that is less than zero. For example, -9 is a negative number.

_n_-gon: A general polygon with "n" number of sides.

Nonagon: A polygon with nine sides.

Number line: A line on which every point represents a real number.

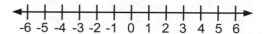

Numerator: The top number of a fraction. For example, 4 is the numerator of the fraction $\frac{4}{7}$.

Obtuse angle: An angle with measure between 90° and 180°. See Unit 6 reference page 46 for an example.

Obtuse triangle: A triangle with one obtuse angle. See Unit 6 reference page 47 for an example.

Octagon: A polygon with eight sides.

Operation: Addition, subtraction, multiplication, and division are the four basic arithmetic operations.

Ordered pair: A pair of numbers where order is important. Ordered pairs are used to indicate the location of points on a coordinate plane and are written in the form (*x, y*).

Order of operations: 1) Do all operations within <u>P</u>arentheses; 2) Apply all <u>E</u>xponents; 3) <u>M</u>ultiply and <u>D</u>ivide from left to right; 4) <u>A</u>dd and <u>S</u>ubtract from left to right. (PEMDAS).

Origin: The point of intersection of the *x*-axis and the *y*-axis on a coordinate graph identified by the point (0, 0). See the coordinate graph on page 44 for an example.

Parallel lines: Lines that are in the same plane and never intersect. For example, the lines below are parallel.

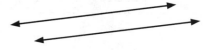

Parallelogram: A quadrilateral with two pairs of parallel sides. The figure below is a parallelogram.

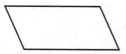

Pentagon: A polygon with five sides. See Unit 6 reference page 48 for an example.

Percent of change: A measure of how a value changes in relation to the original value. For example, an increase from $10 to $15 represents a 50% change.

Percent of decrease: A measure of how a value has decreased in relation to the original value. For example, a decrease from $40 to $10 represents a 75% decrease.

Percent of increase: A measure of how a value has increased in relation to the original value. For example, an increase from $20 to $25 represents a 25% increase.

Percent: A ratio that compares a number to 100. Percent means *per hundred* and is represented by the symbol %. For example, the ratio 25 to 100 can be written as 25%.

Perpendicular lines: Two lines that form a right angle. The two perpendicular lines below meet to form a right angle.

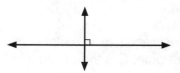

Perimeter: The distance around a figure. For example, the perimeter of the triangle is 30 cm.

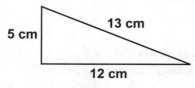

Pi (π): The ratio of the circumference of a circle to its diameter. π is $\frac{22}{7}$, which is often shortened to about 3.14. π has not been solved.

Plane: A flat surface with no thickness that continues without end in all directions. A plane can be named using four letters or just one. See Unit 6 reference page 46 for an example.

Point: Represents a position in space. Capital letters are used to name points. See Unit 6 reference page 46 for an example.

Polygon: A closed figure that has three or more sides. Each side is a line segment, and the sides meet only at the endpoints, or vertices. See Unit 6 reference pages 47 and 48 for examples.

Positive number: A number that is greater than zero. For example, 7 is a positive number.

Prime Number: A number whose only factors are 1 and the number itself. For example, 7 is a prime number, because 1 and 7 are its only factors.

Prism: A three-dimensional shape with two congruent parallel bases. All other sides are rectangles. For example, the solids below are prisms.

Probability: The chance that a particular outcome will occur.

Product: The result of a multiplication problem. For example, 6 is the product in 2 x 3 = 6.

Proportion: An equation formed by two equal ratios. For example, the following is a proportion.
$$\frac{2}{3} = \frac{4}{6}$$

Pythagorean theorem: A theorem that shows a special relationship between the three sides of a right triangle. It says that the sum of the squares of the two legs of a right triangle is equal to the square of the hypotenuse. The relationship is represented by the equation $a^2 + b^2 = c^2$.

Quadrilateral: A polygon with four sides. See Unit 6 reference page 48 for an example.

Quotient: The result of a division problem. For example, 5 is the quotient in 10 ÷ 2 = 5.

Radius: A segment joining the center of the circle to any point on the circle.

Ratio: A comparison of two numbers. The ratio 2 to 3 can also be written as 2:3 or $\frac{2}{3}$.

Ray: Part of a line with one endpoint. A ray continues without end in one direction. The endpoint and one additional point are used to name a ray. See Unit 6 reference page 46 for an example.

Reciprocals: Two numbers that have a product of 1. For example, $\frac{3}{5}$ and $\frac{5}{3}$ are reciprocals, because $\frac{3}{5} \times \frac{5}{3} = 1$.

Rectangle: A quadrilateral that has four right angles. For example, the figure below is a rectangle.

Rectangular prism: A solid figure with congruent rectangular bases and faces that are parallelograms. The figure below is a rectangular prism.

Reflection: A type of transformation that makes a mirror image of the original figure by flipping it over a line. See Unit 6 reference page 49 for an example.

Reflex angle: An angle with measure greater than 180°. See Unit 6 reference page 46 for an example.

Remainder: The number left over when one number does not divide evenly into another number. For example, 3 is the remainder of 35 ÷ 4.

Right angle: An angle with measure equal to 90°. See Unit 6 reference page 46 for an example.

Right triangle: A triangle with one right angle. See Unit 6 reference page 47 for an example.

Rotation: A type of transformation that turns a figure around a point by a certain angle. See Unit 6 reference page 49 for an example.

Sample space: A list of all possible outcomes.

Scale factor: A ratio relating the corresponding sides of two similar figures. For example, the scale factor of the similar triangles below is 2:1.

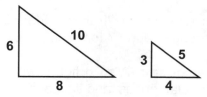

Scalene triangle: A triangle with no sides equal in length. See Unit 6 reference page 47 for an example.

Scientific notation: A number written as the product of a number between 1 and 10 and a power of ten; used to simplify working with very large or very small numbers. For example, 3.2×10^8 is 320,000,000 written in scientific notation.

Segment: Part of a line with two endpoints. Two points are used to name a segment. See Unit 6 reference page 46 for an example.

Similar figures: Two or more figures that have the same *shape*, but are not necessarily the same *size*. For example, the triangles below are similar.

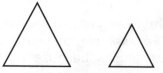

Slope: The measure of the steepness of a line.

Use the ratio $\dfrac{\text{rise}}{\text{run}}$ or

$$\dfrac{\text{difference in } y\text{-coordinates}}{\text{difference in } x\text{-coordinates}}$$

to calculate the slope of a line.

Square: A quadrilateral with four right angles and four equal sides. The figure below is a square.

Squaring: Raising a number to the second power. For example, 3^2 is 3 squared.

Square Root: The opposite of the square of a number. Finding the number that, when squared, equals the number under the radical sign. For example, the square root of 16, or $\sqrt{16}$, is 4.

Stem-and-leaf plot: A diagram that uses place value to organize data. See Unit 7 reference page 64 for an example.

Straight angle: An angle with a measurement equal to 180°. See Unit 6 reference page 46 for an example.

Standard System: A system of measurement that is not based on powers of ten. Feet, pounds, and gallons are examples of standard units of measurement. See Unit 6 reference page 49 for more examples.

Sum: The result of an addition problem. For example, the sum of 3 and 4 is 7.

Supplementary angles: Angles that have a sum of 180°. For example, angles A and B are supplementary angles, because 120° + 60° = 180°.

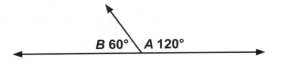

B 60° *A* 120°

Surface Area: The total area of the exterior surfaces of a solid figure.

Symmetric figure: A figure that can be folded in half so that the two halves match. See Unit 6 reference page 48 for an example.

Term: A number, variable, or a number and a variable combined with multiplication or division. For example, $3x^5$, $4xy$, and 5 are all terms in the expression $3x^5 + 4xy + 5$.

Third quartile (Q3): The median of the second half of a data set. For example, 12 is the third quartile of the data set 2, 3, 5, 8, 9, 12, 13.

Transformation: The movement of a figure in a plane. See Unit 6 reference page 49 for an example.

Translation: A type of transformation that slides a figure in a given direction for a certain distance. See Unit 6 reference page 49 for an example.

Transversal: A line that intersects two other lines. For example, line *p* is a transversal.

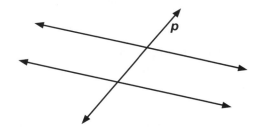

Trapezoid: A quadrilateral with exactly one pair of opposite sides parallel. The figure below is a trapezoid.

Tree diagram: A diagram that is shaped like a tree and is used to show the outcomes of an experiment. For example, the diagram below is a tree diagram that shows the number of possible outfits you can make with a pair of jeans and four different shirts.

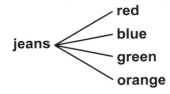

jeans — red, blue, green, orange

Triangle: A polygon with three sides. See Unit 6 reference page 47 for examples.

Triangular prism: A solid figure with congruent triangular bases and faces that are parallelograms. The figure below is a triangular prism.

Variable: A symbol (usually a letter) that stands for an unknown number. For example, z is a variable in the expression $8z - 2$.

Vertex (plural: vertices): The point where two rays of an angle meet or two sides of a polygon meet. For example, point B is the vertex of angle ABC and point X is one vertex of polygon $WXYZ$.

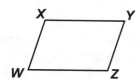

Vertical angles: Angles that are opposite each other. Vertical angles have the same measure. For example, angles 1 and 2 are vertical angles.

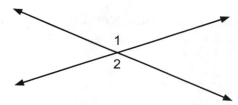

Volume: How much a container can hold in cubic units. For example, the volume of the rectangular prism below is 60 in.^{3}.

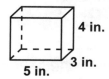

4 in.

3 in.

5 in.

x-axis: The horizontal axis on a coordinate graph. See the coordinate graph on page 44 for an example.

x-coordinate: The first number in an ordered pair that gives the horizontal location of a point. For example, in the ordered pair (3, 2), the number 3 is the x-coordinate.

y-axis: The vertical axis on a coordinate graph. See the coordinate graph on page 44 for an example.

y-coordinate: The second number in an ordered pair that gives the vertical location of a point. For example, in the ordered pair (-5, 6), the number 6 is the y-coordinate.

Answer Keys

Unit 1: Decimals
Lesson 1: Adding Decimals (page 4)
1. 50.8   **2.** 119.524   **3.** 21.0127
4. 45.16   **5.** 384.688   **6.** 14.303
7. 47.1298   **8.** 532.4947

Lesson 2: Subtracting Decimals (page 5)
1. 7.3   **2.** 38.123   **3.** 101.03
4. 21.61   **5.** 126.447   **6.** 2.47
7. 23.1499   **8.** 8.699

Lesson 3: Multiplying Decimals (page 7)
1. 522.405   **2.** 96.775
3. 7.70231   **4.** 1,951.04
5. 1.1812910   **6.** 8,761,103.0
7. 3,116.15983   **8.** 3.4389
9. 291.05   **10.** 513.976
11. 1.601488   **12.** 243.75
13. 122.494   **14.** 45.934
15. 7.3968   **16.** 9,073.0
17. 38.61608   **18.** 49.24641

Lesson 4: Dividing Decimals (page 9)
1. 3.8   **2.** 6.7   **3.** 15
4. 8.6   **5.** 16.4   **6.** 6.7
7. 23.41   **8.** 3.25   **9.** 32.875
10. 5.6   **11.** 2.89   **12.** 4.65
13. 17   **14.** 11.3   **15.** 2
16. 26

Unit 2: Pre-Algebra
Lesson 5: Factors and Greatest Common Factor (page 10)
1. T   **2.** F   **3.** F   **4.** T
5. 4   **6.** 15   **7.** 5   **8.** 8

Lesson 6: Prime Factorization (page 11)
1. $2 \times 2 \times 3 \times 5$ **2.** $2 \times 2 \times 5 \times 5$
3. $2 \times 3 \times 11$ **4.** Prime
5. 2×41 **6.** 2×19
7. $2 \times 2 \times 2 \times 2 \times 2 \times 2$ **8.** Prime
9. $2 \times 3 \times 3 \times 5$
10. $2 \times 2 \times 2 \times 2 \times 2 \times 2 \times 5$

Lesson 7: Multiples and Least Common Multiple (page 12)
1. 6, 12, 18, 24, 30   **2.** 14, 28, 42, 56, 70
3. 63   **4.** 30   **5.** 90
6. 72   **7.** 60   **8.** 72

Lesson 8: Exponents and Properties of Exponents (page 14)
1. 4^5 **2.** 10^7 **3.** $3^3 \times 6^2$
4. $8^4 \times 5^4$ **5.** 1   **6.** 4
7. 9^8 **8.** 5^{18} **9.** 8^7
10. 7^{18} **11.** 7^2 **12.** 4^{10}

Lesson 9: Order of Operations (page 15)
1. 62   **2.** 0   **3.** 42   **4.** 34
5. 8   **6.** 6   **7.** 27   **8.** 3
9. 18   **10.** 1

Lesson 10: Square Roots and Approximating Square Roots (page 16)
1. 4   **2.** 8   **3.** 10   **4.** 9
5. between 4 and 5
6. between 8 and 9
7. between 10 and 11
8. between 2 and 3
9. 4.583   **10.** 8.062
11. 10.198   **12.** 2.646

Lesson 11: Scientific Notation (page 17)
1. 7.3×10^4 **2.** 6.2×10^7
3. 8.21×10^5 **4.** 3.7×10^{-5}
5. 3.9×10^{-4} **6.** 7×10^{-7}
7. 240,000   **8.** 49,000,000
9. 74,300   **10.** 0.0000049
11. 0.00203   **12.** 0.00008

Lesson 12: Variables and Evaluating Expressions (page 18)
1. 1   **2.** 8   **3.** -30
4. 1   **5.** 2   **6.** -12

Lesson 13: Simplifying Expressions (page 19)
1. $6z$ **2.** $7x$ **3.** $13y$ **4.** $-2a$
5. $5a + 3b$ **6.** $30k$
7. $13x + 20$ **8.** $13w + 8x$
9. $8n + 14$ **10.** $-35x$
11. $15m + 18$ **12.** $14a + 15b + 24$

Unit 3: Fractions and Mixed Numbers
Lesson 14: Equivalent Fractions (page 20)
Answers may vary for each of these exercises. Several possible answers have been provided.

1. $\frac{4}{6}, \frac{6}{9}, \frac{10}{15}$ **2.** $\frac{2}{3}, \frac{28}{42}, \frac{42}{63}$

3. $\frac{6}{8}, \frac{9}{12}, \frac{15}{20}$ 4. $\frac{3}{4}, \frac{9}{12}, \frac{18}{24}$

5. $\frac{10}{16}, \frac{15}{24}, \frac{25}{40}$ 6. $\frac{18}{25}, \frac{36}{50}, \frac{144}{200}$

Lesson 15: Simplest Form (page 21)

1. $\frac{4}{5}$ 2. $\frac{5}{9}$ 3. $\frac{2}{3}$ 4. $\frac{8}{15}$

5. $\frac{2}{3}$ 6. $\frac{3}{8}$ 7. $\frac{8}{9}$ 8. $\frac{5}{6}$ 9. $\frac{13}{15}$

Lesson 16: Adding and Subtracting Fractions With Like Denominators (page 22)

1. $\frac{3}{5}$ 2. $\frac{5}{7}$ 3. $\frac{1}{2}$ 4. $\frac{9}{11}$

5. $\frac{1}{3}$ 6. $\frac{4}{7}$ 7. $\frac{3}{5}$ 8. $\frac{1}{3}$

Lesson 17: Adding and Subtracting Mixed Numbers With Like Denominators (page 23)

1. $7\frac{2}{3}$ 2. $10\frac{4}{7}$ 3. $12\frac{1}{4}$ 4. $11\frac{8}{13}$

5. $5\frac{2}{3}$ 6. $2\frac{3}{7}$ 7. $6\frac{3}{11}$ 8. $5\frac{1}{5}$

Lesson 18: Adding and Subtracting Fractions With Unlike Denominators (page 24)

1. $\frac{7}{10}$ 2. $\frac{7}{9}$ 3. $\frac{19}{48}$ 4. $\frac{5}{12}$

5. $\frac{1}{2}$ 6. $\frac{2}{3}$ 7. $\frac{5}{12}$ 8. $\frac{23}{35}$

Lesson 19: Adding and Subtracting Mixed Numbers With Unlike Denominators and No Regrouping (page 25)

1. $8\frac{9}{20}$ 2. $6\frac{19}{24}$ 3. $12\frac{3}{4}$ 4. $13\frac{11}{15}$

5. $10\frac{1}{4}$ 6. $8\frac{1}{2}$ 7. $1\frac{3}{10}$ 8. $3\frac{7}{36}$

Lesson 20: Multiplying Fractions (page 26)

1. $\frac{3}{8}$ 2. $\frac{5}{8}$ 3. $\frac{5}{18}$ 4. $\frac{3}{22}$

5. $\frac{3}{8}$ 6. $\frac{16}{63}$ 7. $\frac{4}{25}$ 8. $\frac{1}{4}$

Lesson 21: Dividing Fractions (page 27)

1. $\frac{5}{6}$ 2. $\frac{5}{7}$ 3. $\frac{5}{7}$ 4. $\frac{10}{13}$

5. $\frac{15}{22}$ 6. $\frac{6}{17}$ 7. $\frac{2}{5}$ 8. $\frac{11}{18}$

Lesson 22: Improper Fractions and Mixed Numbers (page 28)

1. $3\frac{3}{5}$ 2. $6\frac{3}{4}$ 3. $4\frac{1}{8}$ 4. $8\frac{5}{6}$

5. $\frac{7}{3}$ 6. $\frac{35}{8}$ 7. $\frac{53}{16}$ 8. $\frac{131}{12}$

Lesson 23: Adding Mixed Numbers With Regrouping (page 29)

1. $9\frac{2}{5}$ 2. $10\frac{1}{7}$ 3. $6\frac{1}{3}$

4. $8\frac{2}{9}$ 5. $6\frac{7}{48}$ 6. $4\frac{59}{72}$

Lesson 24: Subtracting Mixed Numbers With Regrouping (page 30)

1. $2\frac{2}{3}$ 2. $3\frac{1}{2}$ 3. $6\frac{3}{5}$

4. $2\frac{3}{20}$ 5. $1\frac{19}{24}$ 6. $3\frac{7}{18}$

Lesson 25: Multiplying Mixed Numbers (page 31)

1. $15\frac{1}{8}$ 2. $10\frac{5}{7}$ 3. $9\frac{5}{8}$

4. $16\frac{16}{35}$ 5. $18\frac{5}{12}$ 6. $24\frac{29}{63}$

Lesson 26: Dividing Mixed Numbers (page 32)

1. $1\frac{23}{40}$ 2. $\frac{47}{57}$ 3. $1\frac{17}{35}$

4. $\frac{57}{155}$ 5. $\frac{41}{84}$ 6. $2\frac{27}{32}$

Unit 4: Ratio, Proportion, and Percents
Lesson 27: Ratio and Proportion (page 33)

1. $\frac{14}{12}$ or $\frac{7}{6}$ 2. $\frac{12}{14}$ or $\frac{6}{7}$

3. $\frac{14}{26}$ or $\frac{7}{13}$ 4. $\frac{26}{12}$ or $\frac{13}{6}$

5. =, yes   6. ≠, no
7. ≠, no   8. =, yes

Lesson 28: Solving Proportions (page 35)
1. $x = 28$
2. $a = 20$
3. $b = 14$
4. $y = 32$
5. $w = 24$
6. $4.00
7. 80 yds.
8. 45 times
9. $6.00
10. 5 gallons

Lesson 29: Similar Figures and Scale Factor (page 36)
1. Yes; 2
2. No
3. Yes; 3
4. No

Lesson 30: Fractions and Percents (page 37)
1. 23% 2. 58% 3. 30% 4. 28%
5. $\frac{1}{4}$ 6. $\frac{3}{5}$ 7. $\frac{1}{20}$ 8. $\frac{9}{20}$

Lesson 31: Decimals and Percents (page 38)
1. 33%
2. 6%
3. 70%
4. 68%
5. 36%
6. 0.2%
7. 63%
8. 37.5%
9. 0.47
10. 0.5
11. 0.05
12. 1
13. 0.275
14. 0.0125
15. 0.36
16. 0.01

Lesson 32: Using and Finding Percents (page 39)
1. 60
2. 665
3. 10.8
4. 27
5. 25%
6. 48%
7. 15%
8. 10%
9. 20
10. 60
11. 50
12. 375

Lesson 33: Percent Increase and Decrease (page 40)
1. 32%
2. 19%
3. 84%
4. 75%
5. 98%
6. 2%
7. 17%
8. 53%
9. 30%
10. 16%
11. 11%
12. 50%

Unit 5: Integers
Lesson 34: Adding integers (page 41)
1. 4
2. -38
3. -6
4. 6
5. 24
6. -12
7. -2
8. -11

Lesson 35: Subtracting Integers (page 42)
1. 22
2. 18
3. -23
4. 32
5. -12
6. -21
7. -86
8. 25

Lesson 36: Multiplying and Dividing Integers (page 43)
1. negative
2. positive
3. positive
4. negative
5. positive
6. negative

7. -7
8. -48
9. 12
10. -45
11. 65
12. -6

Lesson 37: Coordinate Graphs (page 45)
1. (-5, 7)
2. (-8, -3)
3. (9, 0)
4. (8, 5)
5. (0, -3)
6. (1, -4)
7.–12.   See graph

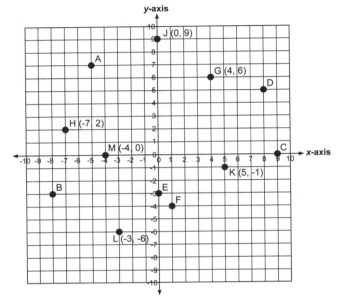

Unit 6: Geometry
Lesson 38: Perimeter (page 50)
1. 24 cm
2. 34 in.
3. 60 ft.

Lesson 39: Circumference (page 51)
1. 87.92 m
2. 28.26 ft.
3. 50.24 in.
4. 7.85 cm
5. 43.96 in.
6. 40.82 cm
7. 84.78 m
8. 23.55 ft.

Lesson 40: Area of Rectangles and Parallelograms (page 52)
1. 56 ft.^{2}
2. 30 cm^2
3. 56 in.^{2}
4. 52.5 m^2

Lesson 41: Area of Triangles (page 53)
1. 12 cm^2
2. 67.5 m^2
3. 60 in.^{2}

Lesson 42: Area of Trapezoids (page 54)
1. 16 cm^2
2. 63 ft.^{2}
3. 180 in.^{2} or 1.25 ft.^{2}

Lesson 43: Area of Circles (page 55)
1. 28.26 ft.^{2}
2. 314 m^2
3. 2,826 cm^2
4. 3.14 in.^{2}

Lesson 44: Surface Area of Rectangular and Triangular Prisms (page 56)
1. 126 ft.²   2. 56 m²   3. 108 cm²
4. 127 in.²

Lesson 45: Surface Area of Cylinders (page 58)
1. 244.92 cm²   2. 276.32 m²
3. 527.52 in.²

Lesson 46: Volume (page 59)
1. $V = 401.92$ ft.³   2. $V = 160$ yd.³
3. $V = 1,099$ mm³

Lesson 47: Pythagorean Theorem (page 60)
1. $c = 10$ ft.   2. $a = 10$ yd.
3. $c = 17$ mm   4. $b = 24$ cm

Lesson 48: Angle Relationships and Intersecting Lines (page 61)
1. $a = 145°, b = 35°, c = 145°$
2. $a = 28°, b = 152°, c = 28°$

Lesson 49: Angle Relationships and Parallel Lines (page 62)
1. 36°   2. 144°   3. 36°   4. 144°
5. 36°   6. 144°

Unit 7: Probability and Statistics
Lesson 50: Measures of Central Tendency (page 65)
1. mean = 7, median = 6, mode = 6
2. mean = 4, median = 3, mode = 2
3. mean = 6, median = 6, mode = 5

Lesson 51: Possible Outcomes (page 66)
1. 9   2. 18   3. 12

Lesson 52: Simple Probability (page 67)
1. $P(2) = \frac{3}{8}$ 2. $P(\text{odd}) = \frac{3}{8}$
3. $P(\text{less than 5}) = \frac{5}{8}$

Lesson 53: Independent and Dependent Events (page 69)
1. independent; $\frac{2}{121}$ 2. dependent; $\frac{3}{55}$
3. independent; $\frac{8}{121}$ 4. dependent; $\frac{2}{55}$
5. independent; $\frac{1}{12}$ 6. independent; $\frac{1}{4}$

Unit 8: Linear Equations
Lesson 54: Solving One-Step Equations by Adding and Subtracting (page 70)
1. $x = 25$ 2. $a = 11$ 3. $g = -67$
4. $b = 53$ 5. $p = 65$ 6. $n = -5$
7. $v = 108$ 8. $c = -19$ 9. $x = -18$

Lesson 55: Solving One-Step Equations by Multiplying and Dividing (page 71)
1. $x = 6$ 2. $p = 16$ 3. $h = -4$
4. $d = -10$ 5. $m = 52$ 6. $b = 720$
7. $w = -24$ 8. $x = -15$

Lesson 56: Solving Two-Step Equations (page 72)
1. $t = 3$ 2. $p = 2$ 3. $n = -7$
4. $x = 3$ 5. $y = 40$ 6. $b = 75$
7. $n = 28$ 8. $a = -4$

Lesson 57: Graphing Linear Equations (page 74)
1.
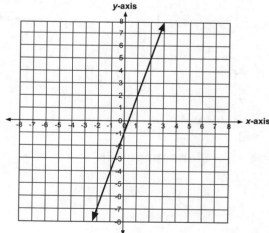
2.
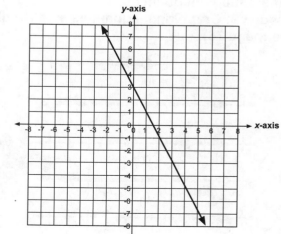

3.

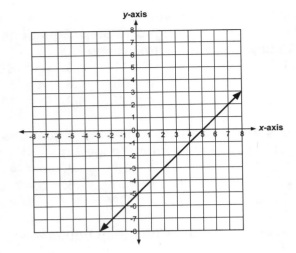

4.

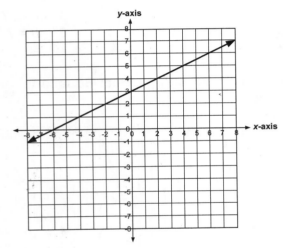

Lesson 58: Slope (page 75)

1. -1   **2.** $\frac{3}{2}$ **3.** $-\frac{1}{2}$ **4.** $\frac{1}{3}$

5. 0   **6.** no slope

Unit 9: Linear Inequalities
Lesson 59: Graphing Inequalities on a Number Line (page 76)

1.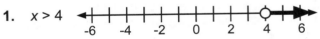

2.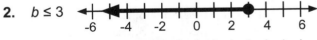

3.

4.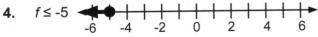

5.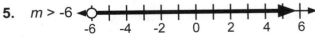

6.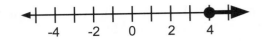

Lesson 60: Solving One-Step Inequalities by Adding and Subtracting (page 77)

1. $x \le 1$

2. $b > 4$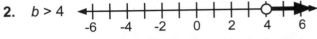

3. $d \ge -4$

4. $w < -5$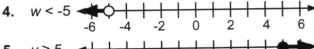

5. $y \ge 5$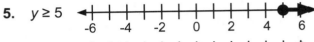

6. $p \le 6$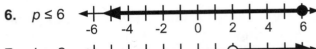

7. $h > 2$

8. $n \ge -5$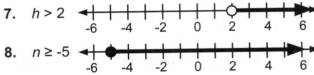

Lesson 61: Solving One-Step Inequalities by Multiplying and Dividing (page 78)

1. $x > 4$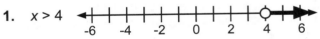

2. $b \le 3$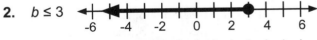

3. $c < 4$

4. $f \le -5$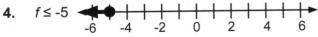

5. $m > -6$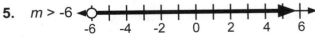

6. $t \le -2$

7. $d > -4$

8. $x < 3$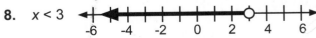